Best Wishes
Cindy Be

All the Best
wee Frank.

If Your Feet Are Tired And Weary

A Childhood memory of a young boy growing up in the West of Glasgow...Known simply to many as the land of Temple Scurvy

Andy Bell

AuthorHouse™ UK Ltd.
500 Avebury Boulevard
Central Milton Keynes, MK9 2BE
www.authorhouse.co.uk
Phone: 08001974150

© *2009 Andy Bell. All rights reserved.*

No part of this book may be reproduced, stored in a retrieval system, or transmitted by any means without the written permission of the author.

First published by AuthorHouse 5/14/2009

ISBN: 978-1-4389-7954-0 (sc)

This book is printed on acid-free paper.

The cover photo, showing the Forth and Clyde Canal at Temple, Glasgow, was taken in August 2007 by Douglas MacGregor who retains the copyright and all rights to the photograph. It is reproduced here by permission."

Dedication

This book is dedicated to my big sister Catherine who will always remain alive in my heart and memories. Also to all those people who throughout the years listened to my short stories about my life and times growing up in Temple and spending many hours laughing their heeds aff, listening and encouraging me to write the stories down. I'm also inspired by the suggestion that the best days of your life are *growing up*. For me, it was the importance of capturing many magical memories, ups and downs, happy and sad stories, but never a dull day and being brought up in a place blessed with characters, hard-working families and a neighbourhood that had a real strength of community, like a big extended family associated for life, simply for living, growing up, or choosing to hang about the land, known to many as *Temple Scurvy*.

And finally a big thanks to all our neighbours that tapped us milk, breed and sugar on a regular basis.... including the one's who were always kidden on they were oot....

Contents

- Introduction 1
- Someone is missing 7
- The family and neighbours 10
- A day at the circus 12
- Old Jack 17
- Indoor camping 21
- Bits and Bobs of how it was 24
- Collecting gingee's 35
- Boundaries 38
- Glasgow Fair 41
- Oh! Mammy! Daddy! 43
- The Nolly 45
- Dossy Park 49
- Truth, derr, double derr, promise or command 53
- Jacques Cousteau 55
- Hacked off 64
- The Night auld Dixie came to town? 66
- Buzzing 68
- From Big Shaggy to Stan laurel 79
- Any Extras (school) 81
- The Big School 98
- Bogeys, Crossbows and a Dodgy bike 122
- It's bigger than a dug 134
- Two cans, bottle of cider and the Grease Album 138
- The Berries (Blairgowerie) 142
- Breed, Coal and a Sugar strike 150

- Being the boss's son   154
- Michael No butter Cairney   160
- Hail Hail in the jail   164
- He's leaving us   172

If your feet are tired and weary

By

Andy Bell

Acknowledgments

I would like to express my gratitude to the many people who saw me through this book; to all those who provided support, talked things over, read, offered comments and allowed me to write about our stories growing up together in Temple.

I would like to thank Authors house for enabling me to publish this book. Above all I want to thank my wife, Joyce for all her support and patience including the late nights, endless questions of "what if? Or "what do you think? And to the rest of my family, who supported and encouraged me to make this book a reality.

Last and not least: I ask forgiveness of all those who have been with me over the course of the years and whose names I have failed to mention."

Introduction

If your feet are tired and weary and your heart has missed a beat you'll get your fucken head kicked in if you walk down Fulton Street, take a stroll into the siggy and you'll here a famous cry, get out ya dirty bastards we're the Temple Scurvy boy's and the song goes on. They also used to sing "Hi Ho Temple Scurvy" they were the big team. I was a young young scurvy boy (YYTS) for menshie purposes all written interlinked.

For the record the biggest mention I got was done by a large roller and tray in loud yellow paint, "Nosher", up at the nolly on the side wall off Bearsden road. A razzer so all the Drum boys could see it from the blue bus, it was easy five foot high, and it lasted years.

For me it all began in 1963, 28th August to be exact the same day in America a march for civil rights and freedom in which Martin Luther King delivered his historical " *I have a dream"* speech in Washington DC and *Bad to me* by Billy J. Kramer was top of the charts. I reckon the headlines belonged to Martin Luther King that day and now I understand why I never made the news.

I was born in Redlands maternity hospital in Glasgow, I was named after my uncle Andy with Joseph attached in the middle, but I could never say Joseph it was always Andrew Joffus Bell. For the first

Andy Bell

6 months of my life I lived in Whiteinch near Partick in the West End of Glasgow. The flat in which we lived in had one bedroom which was famously known in Glasgow as a '*single en*' *with* the outside toilet shared by all the neighbours up the tenement close.

We left the coal bunker with windows in Whiteinch and moved to Temple into a four apartment tenement, the house seemed enormous it had 3 bedrooms, living room, separate kitchen and bathroom with six houses up the close 3 high, 32 Willow street, bottom right to be exact, at this stage in the Bell family there was five of us, mum, dad, myself, big sister by 2 years Catherine and "moon dog" (John) my young and only brother.

When I was just 2 years old Some big arsehole who lived across the back court from us fired a caterpillar sling with glass in it, at me when I was playing, it stuck in my face and scarred me for life, my parents told me they never got the bastard, but they had an idea who it was but couldn't prove it, what a start to life in Temple, *chibbed* when I was a toddler, hard to believe, but unfortunately all very true.

Temple is an old district of Glasgow, in the North West of the city, bounded by Anniesland to the south, Knightswood to the west and Kelvindale to the east. The name comes from a place of worship established in the settlement by the Knights Templar in or around the 12th century.

Temple, like many of Glasgow's suburbs, was originally a village of its own, and was swallowed by Glasgow's expansion in the late 19th and early 20th centuries. It was annexed by Glasgow in 1912. Mills were the primary employers in the old village. It is linked to maryhill via the Forth and Clyde canal.

The official gang title was *Temple Scurvy;* I remember being told that someone once wrote in a book that in the late sixties Temple scurvy ruled Barlinnie prison. Me and my mates thought this story was amazing; such a small place with the population being a few thousand depending where you thought Temple started and finished.

The main employers in the area were Dunn the sawmill (the widdy), Caullers the commercial cleaners, the buses, the coal, Sloan's dairy, Barr and Stroud, Morton's (the world famous roll maker), Ciro plastics the cellotape factory on Succoth Rd and the shipyards, most of our parents worked in one of these places or they were window cleaners or Nolly bum's, home brewers, part-time gamblers or full time domino players with a permanent seat in the local boozers the den which was in *the linden* or the *siggy,* the signal box.

One of my youngest memories was a time I put the boot into my uncle Shug, it was his wedding day, and he was marrying my mum's sister *Georgie.* Shug had a large family *the Murray's; they* lived in the tenement facing ours, the top floor flat known in Glasgow as a tap dancer. I believe the wedding reception was held

Andy Bell

in Shug's ma's hoose across the street, no fancy big hall's or buffets on offer. Just lots of dodgy chocolate brown pin stripe suits, high waster trousers, snake belts, platform shoes and feather cut hair doo's, the kind of suits you couldn't put the iron over the nylon trousers without burning the arse out them and not forgetting the iron was kept on the stove, solid metal all over including the handle, very easy to burn your hands off.

The Murray's were all six feet tall, no girls in the family (6) brothers; Kevin shared the same birthday as me so Mrs Murray used to give me a wee bung on my birthday. I must have been at the wedding with my parents, I remember I was kept in the kitchen or *scullery* which was the old fashioned name for a kitchen, it had a stove built into the wall with a hatch straight through to the living room. I was missing the action so I was playing up outside in the hall when Shug got a hold of my arms to try and calm me down, I was having none of it I wanted my mum and dad. So I decided to boot Shug in the shin, he held in his painful scream by covering his mouth, it was an unexpected kick and didn't amuse him, he closed the living room door and dished out 10 rapid onto my backside.

I don't recall receiving a Christmas present from Shug after the incident, Shug always reminds me of that day. Its strange how families develop, Shug had all brothers and auntie Georgie was desperate for a daughter and ended up with 4 boys, Shug blamed it on his ma's home made lentil soup.

My auntie Georgie liked taking my sister Catherine out in her pram she spent a lot of time with her having wee shots of dressing her up with nice wee baby girl clothes and hoping one day she and Shug would have their own wee daughter.

My mum and Georgie are very close they both had a bit of a difficult time growing up, I believe they both were brought up by their aunties due to my grannies new man not wanting much to do with another man's children. However, my mum and Georgie remained very close to my grannie and to their new brothers and sisters they included John, Alex, Twins David and Margaret, William and Ellen, known as Cammie, she was closest to me by age and hung about with me, they simply all seen themselves as one big family and nothing step about them. I think my granda mellowed towards my mum and Georgia through time. He was a difficult man my granda a real Jekyll and Hyde, his mood swings and temperament were all over the place especially towards my gran. Sadly my grannie is no longer with us, she was known as *Nellie* I loved her very much and miss not having her around, she was a great woman *(apart from putting butter beans in her homemade soup)* she was hard working, kind, and a great support for my mum. I think she got on okay with my dad, put up with him for my mum's sake and to keep the peace.

Andy Bell

My dad's big brother Andy also stayed in Temple, he was married to Theresa, they had 4 weans, Norman, Andrew, Stephen and young Theresa, unfortunately my uncle Andy died at 44 he suffered a heart attack and passed away in Temple near his house, I also miss him, he and my dad were so funny together, especially telling their stories of growing up, they would laugh for hours at a time, however, his spirit lives on via his family who have inherited his great sense of humour.

I suppose to the outside world, we were considered *a poor wee family* with lots of young weans and lacking in modern clothes and material items, but in reality everybody was skint and got tick from the shops. It's hard to explain that you may look poor in some ways but feel very rich in many other ways, friends and adventure, internally happy and glad to feel and be part of something and somewhere very special, I suppose I was very happy with all my family, I loved going to my grannies and had really good pals.

Someone is missing

I remember being taken off to my grannies she lived in Hawick Street in Yoker. I was around 3 years old; my brother John was 2 years old and my sister Brenda was 8 months. I was at my grannies for what felt like ages. I didn't know where everyone else was.

What happened on the 5th August 1966 would have a bearing on our family for the rest of our lives. Catherine was weeks away from starting school, I understand my dad had taken her for new clothes for starting school; Catherine was playing outside the close at the front with a sweeping brush, when she wandered onto the pavement and then the road and was knocked down by a Sloans milk van. The driver was a young guy dating our neighbour's daughter. I only remember adults screaming and crying and people not letting my mum out to the street to get to her wean, Catherine was to die of her injuries shortly that day in hospital. I understand she was very excited about starting school and very pleased with her new school uniform.

What that meant for me was to know and feel someone was missing; no sign of them, no photos or her, no toys or clothes were in the house. I suppose there was fewer photo's around in 1966, and people and families dealt with bereavement differently, the house felt empty and I was all alone, no one to chase and I'm sure it was difficult for my parents when I must have asked them continuously *'where's Caffreen?*

The local priest came to our door after Catherine had died to offer comfort via faith to my mum and dad, but when he suggested to my dad, Catherine has been chosen by God to be an angel, he didn't last too long in the house after that explanation. I don't think my parents religious beliefs were strengthened by this life changing tragic experience. Due to the blanket of silence on the subject, it's hard to reflect on how as a 3 year old I responded to the loss of my big sister, looking all over the house, asking for her. I have no doubt this experience had an adverse effect on my parents and would test their relationship.

It is sad to think that nothing physical belonging to Catherine exists, to my knowledge! I managed to source one picture of Catherine when she was under one year old and a copy of her birth certificate as a real reminder that Catherine was a real person and very much part of our family. I have always wondered who Catherine would have looked like as an adult or what it would be like to have a big sister around to boss me about! When I returned home from my grannies I remember feeling someone's missing, my parents were totally heart broken and they must have cried over and over but hid their grief from us. I often wondered why they never left that house considering every time they went outside they had the visual reminder of where Catherine last played, however,

I understand the importance of having friends and family around you during such a challenging time.

The tragic loss of Catherine undoubtedly has had a lasting effect on both my parents and the rest of our family, and although they say time does ease sadness and bring you peace of mind and heart, it would be great to one day feel able to talk about, ask questions and celebrate Catherine's short but important life as very much part of the Bell clan.

The family and neighbours

During my childhood I felt my mum was always pregnant. They eventually had a total of seven weans, Catherine Georgina, there was myself, Andrew Joffus (Joseph), my brother John Aloysius, Brenda Lee, Christina Susan (Tina), Connie Francis and Heather Veronica. I think they got the names for weans from the Kensistas Rock and Roll album. My dad always worked, he was in the building business, he worked for a small family building company, he was always willing to try anything, always fixing objects around the house, on reflection when your so young my dad was probably only changing a fuse on a plug, but I thought he was so special because he could fix things and make them work again. He was always on demand from the neighbours, especially from some of my pals mum's, doing odd jobs and repairing this and that, he was almost as popular as the local *meter driller* who had a run like the window cleaner.

My mum and dad were the same age, a week between their birthdays, my mum never worked after she got married to my dad she was at home trying to hold things together. What I noticed is they very rarely did things together, like messages, going on nights out with friends, I expect it might have been difficult with all the weans in toe.

I remember the Moses basket kept getting painted for each newborn baby, it sat in the living room. We

If Your Feet Are Tired And Weary

always seemed to have a dog in the family we had *Blacky* a black Labrador my dad used to call him a *flea bag*, he was around for most of my childhood, my mum loved the dog, he followed her everywhere, we also had a boxer called Clare, but she got stole, never too be seen again (our very own Shergar). My mum didn't go out much, she was known as *Chrissie* to all the neighbours and wasn't all that great at reading and writing, she caught meningitis when she was in her early teens, she was very ill, missing a lot of school. I believe an old neighbour Mrs Rooney who rared a family upstairs gave my mum a lot of support and helped her out when it got near Friday with a wee tap. Mrs Rooney was very fond of my mum. I think she felt sorry for her in the task she had. I remember the shops gave *tick* with a note. I was in primary 5/6 and was given the task of dictating my mums tick notes, she kept it quiet from my dad so he thought she coped with the wages, all he was worried about was his dinner after work, potatoes, onion and liver or something substantial like that, a dinner always requiring a drink of water.

I used to add a packet of Jaffa cakes and a bottle of Irn Bru to the tick list, I went to the shops and tailed the biscuits and ginger for later, my mum never mentioned the extra cost on the bill, I think most families got tick in the local shops, because that's the way it was and the task was never embarrassing, even when you met your pals in the same shop, it was everyday life.

A day at the circus

A visit to my grannies was as always a real highlight, especially when she had something special planned for me. I used to head to her house in Yoker (the land of Yoker Toi a doo flyers paradise) on a Friday night and stay all weekend; I remember when I learned to travel on the number 11 bus from Anniesland Cross all by myself, my grannie would meet me at the other end at Garscadden primary school, it made me feel a bit grown up travelling on the bus myself asking the bus driver every second stop "*is it time to get off yet?, "naw son sit down the noo, I'll let you know".*

On one weekend visit my grannie informed me she was taking me to the circus on the Saturday morning, but we had to leave the house very early, so it was early to bed on the Friday night, I noticed there was a lot of commotion in the house on the Friday night all my aunties and uncles arguing about clothes, white shirts, fighting for a shot at the iron and the boys polishing their shoes, a real buzz about the house, I was sent to bed early, but could hear them all still giving it laldy. *"Andra! Andra"*! (Old fashioned Scottish for Andrew) That's what my grannies called me, I could hear her shouting on me, *"its time to get up Andra"*, it was about 7am in the morning the boys and lassies were still hyper and loud, I looked at the clothes the boys and lassies had on and it was strange, the girls looked like American cheer leaders and the boys resembled Scottish highland soldier's, they were

If Your Feet Are Tired And Weary

all in red, white and blue, the front door went and it was my uncles mates with a carryout (drink) this was before 8am and they had started boozing, even my granda was joining in with the early bevy session, my grannies never drank, soon it was time to go to the circus. At 8.30am we all headed to Dumbarton road to get on a pre-arranged coach, the bus was full of people with the same red, white and blue clothes on as my aunties and uncles. I said to my grannies *"are they all part of the big circus we're going to see grannies?* she said *"aye"* ok I thought, we headed off on the bus and ended up at Glasgow town centre and more circus people were there with big drums, there was men with big fancy ties with badges on and some with white gloves and a man with a big fancy circus book on top of a purple cushion, it looked as if it belonged to a real fancy house, maybe it belonged to the queen coz her crown was embroidered onto it. I was told to hold my grannies hand tight as a lot of people were starting to appear and starting to sing songs. All the circus people were starting to line up behind each other in long rows, some of them had nice shinny orange scarves on over their jackets with numbers and letters, a right party atmosphere was developing with singing going on all around me. I asked my granny were the circus animals were? I couldn't see the elephants and tigers but grannies said they were at a big park and we had to follow the circus parade through the streets to the park then at the big park we should see the animals. I remembered Dumbo the film and the circus people held a parade

Andy Bell

and went through the town to announce its arrival. I was well excited!

A man at the front was juggling a big stick and throwing it above the street telephone wires and the crowds were all cheering. The people were all out in the streets to welcome the circus to Glasgow. A big heavy man with a huge belly was beating into a big drum which looked as heavy as 4 cases of alpine ginger the man had his name on the front of the drum incase it got mixed up with all the other drums. I think the circus belonged to a guy called Billy because everybody was singing his name.

I was so proud of my aunties and uncles in the circus; they had kept it all very quiet, there was lots of big banners with horses on them, with two people dancing with the poles, going side to side, kidding on to everybody they where going to drop it.

I felt we had walked for miles; some of the other wee kids, like my size were on top of their parents shoulders I didn't want to ask my granny for a shoudery and my granda had disappeared, he was temporary lost, in a bar on route I believe with his purple nose pals, all the ma's and da's were singing and dancing in the street following the circus big parade. Soon we were arriving at the park and all the circus parades had met up together, I understood why the big chubby guy with the drum had his name on the front of it, because there was hundreds of similar big drums in the park all the guys had their names on them incase they got mixed up, everybody was singing and dancing and drinking lots of bevy, even the circus people from Ireland were at the big parade in the park, but I was on a mission I wanted to see the circus animals, but I was so disappointed when my grannies told me the animals were all sick and stayed at home that day.

I was gutted and losing interest quickly, my uncle Alex came to the rescue he appeared with a packed lunch for everybody, sandwiches and juice and fruit, everybody who supported the circus got a packed lunch, he was telling everybody in the park I was his nephew and I was getting lots of money of his pals, the day was starting to get interesting again, soon I had more than a fiver all to myself, I was soon back with my grannies in the park. I said to my granny I would love a shot at loyal John Black's drum, he was sitting near us in the park, it looked bigger than me, so my grannies to make up for the disappointment of the sick circus animals went and asked big John if I could get a shot of his drum and to my amazement he agreed, it was amazing I was singing and banging away "*boom, boom, boom the circus is on its way*" I played the drum until my arm's were falling off.

Soon all the circus people were starting to go onto buses, a lot of the big people were really drunk, me and my grannies got a bus home (granda still missing) it had been a very long day and we were both very tired. I treated me and my grannies to a big bag of chips each and a big bottle of sore belly ginger on the way home, a great end to a fun day at the circus, I

Andy Bell

was ready for bed early after all the walking we did that day, my feet were all sore.

The next day my dad collected me and on the way home in the car he asked me how I enjoyed my stay at grannies. I said it was amazing but it was a shame for all the circus animals being sick, he asked "*what circus animals?* I told him my grannies took me to the circus and we were in the parade, I said we went through the streets singing songs and telling everybody the circus was in town and because we walked so much we were tired we had a rest in the big park. We got a packed lunch and I got a shot of big John's drum, my dad was not very pleased with the circus story and started swearing in the car and saying "*wait till I fucking see that old cunt, circus my fucking arse"* When we got home I never even got the chance to tell my mum about my exciting time at the circus as my dad was shouting, I think my dad was upset he missed the circus.

Old Jack

My granda Jack, my dads oldman came to live with us when we were young he was some man, I think all his family had a shot of hosting him for a while, Easter was pure magic it wasn't just Easter eggs he bought you but the eggs had toys and puzzles inside them, he loved taking us out on the bus to Partick but he liked the bevy too much. One day he took me and my brother John to Partick, he landed us in a small café and went for a wee drink, he left the woman in the café money for ice-cream and sweets for us, we were quite content with this it was a mini adventure on the bus, meeting all his old mates, they used to give you a bung for being old Jacks grandsons.

It was great, but unfortunately old Jack went home to Temple on the bus minus two grandsons, he got drunk and forgot about us, I bet he heard my dad and mum that day, I don't believe I saw Partick for many years after that, it was walking distance trips after that, down to the Top Hat Café at Anniesland Cross, there was only one thing missing on our special trips *old Jacks grandsons bungs.*

Old Jack was a barber to trade, he had all the clippers and tools and brushes, he had a shop at one time, I think it was in the Partick area, I can just imagine what happened to that, he probably went to the pub and forgot about it! He used to get me up early, I shared a fold away *zed bed* with him, every morning we used to go and get the fresh milk from Sloan's dairy in Spencer Street and fresh rolls from Morton's bakeries at the top of Crow road. My grannies Bell (Katie) died before my mum and dad got married but I believe Jack was a well travelled man, Royal Navy in his younger days, he apparently fathered children in England that we know of, and my dad has step family, a step brother with the same name.

I remember I took my grandas dog up to the shops on a leash but the dog bolted and was knocked down and killed. I returned with only the leash, he ran up to Fulton street and carried the dog home and buried it round the back court, he never even shouted at me, I explained what happened and he left it at that. I remember he always had shiney shoes, and dressed very smartly, he used to polish his shoes for ages. I clearly remember the day my granda died, it was a Sunday morning he had just got out the hospital for the weekend, told strictly not to drink any alcohol, but he was having none of that, so he sneaked a bottle into the house and kept going into the room to have wee swigs.

On that fatal morning I woke up early, my dad had left for work, overtime on a site in Partick, I turned to notice his face was all purple, I went into my mums bedroom woke her up and described the situation, me and my mum went back into the room, I remember her saying "*he doesn't look too well*" and I think she meant it, then she says "*I'll go and get Mrs Rooney*

If Your Feet Are Tired And Weary

to see if she knows what's up with him" and that was the end of old Jack Bell, except one thing, his bed!

I recall sometime later my dad built a dart board cupboard from his box part of the fold away bed, it had 2 doors, *"ideal for the dart board"* my dad said, I couldn't believe he had did this with, my granda's, his dads bed!!!

Me and my brother John were given old Jacks room with new beds all to ourselves, we were given a wardrobe and a set of drawers; we also had an old coal fire it was all very exciting. Signs got made instantly for the door No Entry & All Girls Barred except My Ma.

One of the worst things that came from my granda's death was my dad inherited his barber tools and clippers, so overnight my dad became a class one barber. John and I were the ginnie pigs for him in his short career as a barber. For many years we had the *home bowl style haircuts*. I think he changed the bowl to suit the time of year. (Summer & winter haircuts or the stoogies look-alikes)

We used to cut old shoes and cardboard in an attempt to blunt the scissors, this tactic never worked he went onto using big wallpaper scissors in their place.

Having our own room was great; somewhere to go and get peace and quiet, our room had a window into the front garden about five or six feet from the

Andy Bell

ground. Me and moondog used to throw items into the front garden and dreep out the windy to retrieve it with the danger of getting caught with my dad returning home from collecting his sisters from work, the risk was all part of the game, we needed bricks to climb back in the window. We could watch for my dad coming in and pretend to be sleeping.

Indoor camping

All the big team were all going camping to the bluebell woods or jumping the train to Helensburgh but we had no tent and were not allowed to go camping, some of my pals could go overnight with their big brothers and then come back and tell all the ghost stories of the hairy monsters and lions trying to get in their tent during the night. We all sat saying nothing, shiting ourselves and just listening to every detail and we all totally believed the stories; *"fuck that camping"* my pals would say.

During the summer months off school one of my pals got the chance to put up a big tent belonging to his big brother in the back court I think he lived in it the full summer holidays, we all brought biscuits and juice and someone stole a national geographical magazine out the library, it was like a poor mans scud book, all the half naked women from tribes, we all used to laugh and suggest the Big droopy boobs belong to each other mums. Its strange how this fun and laughter leads to inviting the girls into the tent for a game of truth, derr, double derr, I would pull my Boabey out just to break the ice and my pal would show of his sheriff's badge. We were all keen to see real boobs and if we got a wee swatch at a real furry burger it made your summer holidays.

I remember the day me and moondog had this fascination to sleep in a tent on the floor of our bedroom. We got a washing rope from the back court and tied it across the bedroom, single line to the window and the wardrobe door, then we threw the blankets over the rope stretching the sides out and putting down heavy shoes to preserve the tent shape, then we needed food, into the kitchen we went, packets of biscuits and four pieces in margarine and jam together, that was a brilliant packed lunch. We sneaked back into the room and into the tent for the grub up, the food lasted 10 minutes then the hiccups arrived. We soon got bored and started fighting.

John used to take flakies with his tongue hanging out his mouth, gritting his teeth, attacking when he got mad or he used to lift objects and throw them once I broke his temper.

We went into the wardrobe and slid the clothes to one side of the bar we built paper in the other corner like a camp fire then stole matches from the kitchen and lit the fire. Don't ask why a camp fire but we lit the small fire and within seconds the wardrobe was full of smoke and small flames grew and we ran into the living room and lucky for us it was only my mum that was in, "*Fire! Fire in our room*", John was shouting to my mum, "*our camp fire is out of control, the wardrobes on fire*" mum got water and managed to put the fire out.

She cracked up, attacked us with the sweeping brush, I threw John as a sacrifice from under the bed to take the brunt of the brush. When she saw the blankets used for the tent and the state of the room with the smoked damaged clothes and burnt wardrobe she was shouting at the top of her voice, calling us for everything and threatening to tell my old man. The wardrobe never burned straight through but was badly damaged and marked inside. My mum never told on us but made us clear up the campsite. As a punishment she never washed the clothes in the wardrobe they were stinking of smoke and made us wear them, we both walked about smelling like a couple of Arbroath kippers and got slagged off by our pals and the lassies.

I kept telling my pals at school the Smokey smell from my clothes came from lighting big giant fires in Temple, I got away with it for a week, then Moondog told his pals the real indoor camping story and that all our clothes got burnt or smoke damaged, that's when our school pals would sing or humb the bonanza cowboy tune and sing to me and moon *"we were born under the wandering star"* followed by taunts of *"see you ramorra, long John and Tonto"* along with Indian war dancing sounds "hoya heya, hoya hoya heya" when trying to get off the school bus. I told moon he had a mouth the size of the Clyde tunnel the cowboy slagging eventually wore off.

Bits and Bobs of how it was

John and I used to be in our beds at night singing most of the time. I used to sing a drifters song, *'Saturday night at the movies' and* then ask John to complete the chorus, we practiced that song for years. We also did a double act of a Buddy Holly number *'Oh Boy'* using my mums sweeping brushes for mics, we thought we were brilliant at that number; it became a popular request even as we got older.

The girls would laugh at me and Johns singing and then we would get shouted at for keeping them wakened. We never spent anytime with the girls the age gap was quite big and they were pesty wee sisters who played dollies with all their wee mates.

I remember lots of games like scalextrics, compendium set, striker football and garage motor games, we tended to get big games to share, which always caused a riot between us, most of our other games came from our mad huckleberry adventure imaginations. We all looked forward to Friday night that was pay day for my dad, this was chippy night and we went to the fish shop for dinner, no pressure, we all shared a supper of choice then it was Z cars and the Virginian cowboy programme, back in those days it also felt that nationwide lasted 3 hours, it was absolutely boring for children but adults always watched it especially our dad.

When my dad came in from work he got his dinner, and then most times he went for a wee doss on the couch, could we talk or laugh? No way! he used to take flakies for interrupting his sleep, we used to attempt to make each other laugh, it was pure dare devil stuff, we used to nip each other to see who would get caught and get the traditional *"stripped, washed and bed"* punishment. My dad had the *knack* to sleep, listen to the telly and hear us carry on at the same time. It took us many years to discover he must only be resting lightly.

I remember Apollo being on the telly, it was covering the space mission, and it felt as if it lasted years, and it was terrible! I used to wonder why my dad watched the news, then nationwide, it appeared to be very boring and didn't make sense to me, it's interesting as an adult I watch national news, then Scottish news, my own children must share the same thoughts I had during my childhood.

I didn't attend nursery school when I was younger, maybe it was not available plus my mum had children at all different stages, from being pregnant, a child in the pram, a child at her side and two approaching school age, a bit of a handful. My dad just seemed to work, sleep, moan and play darts and enjoy a swally. He mainly socialised himself, my mum stayed at home with the squad unless they attracted a babysitter this was in the form of my mother's brother, Uncle Alex, my dad called him *The Prince* or *Alex the sock*, coz his big toes was always sticking out his socks.

Alex stayed with my grannies in Yoker, he was called in the odd occasion to baby sit. I remember his tactics clear as day, misbehaviour led to the threat of the big bad fire by saying to us *"do you want to go to the bad fire for not going to sleep"?* We used to plead forgiveness and cry out *"not the bad fire, we'll go to sleep, we're already sleeping, please! Not the fire",* we had enough of fire's with our indoor camping experience.

Alex's party piece was tucking his lower legs up across each other and bumping around the living room floor, we thought he was gifted, we told all our friends of this amazing act. Alex eventually came and lived with us when he was older; he started working with my dad on the building site and over time became very much like a big brother to us and part of the Bell family for many years. Alex is no longer with us he died shortly after my grannies died, he was broken hearted about my grannies death, we all miss him, he was such a likeable guy and he was also very close to my mum.

I always remember my dad's pals in and around the house, a few we referred to as *uncle* only to discover when older it was unofficial. My dad went around with James Murray, Shugs older brother; he attended football matches with him and others at the weekend. I remember my dad made home brew and him and James attacked it prematurely and got in a very drunk state. *'Uncle James'* as we titled him used to call me *luggy ears* and he used to threaten to bite my ears off, they were quite big and stuck out, an easy target for a crazy adult full of home brew. I'm happy to say my ears did survive his threats through out his friendship with my dad. Recently after a long illness James passed away, my mum and dad were both saddened.

My dad was an awful man for bringing his pals back to the house for a drink after the 10pm closing time at the pubs. My mum didn't drink except the odd occasion, she had a wee shandy and she didn't smoke, she remained a spectator during these days and was pestered by the drunks to get up and dance when it came to the records going on. Within the close all the neighbours new each other as was within the street and surrounding area, there didn't seem to be many strangers around in those days. Our next-door neighbour for years was Mr Cairney; he lived in the house bottom floor with his son and daughters. I can't ever remember his wife; his son and daughters were between 5 & 10 years older than me.

Mr Cairney was a proud man, kept very much to himself, he worked in the pub trade, I remember I used to go to the shops for him he was always good at tipping, he was a *"keep the change"* man. Mr Cairney was an older man in his late 50's; his family were grown, attending university and out working. I remember we used to play *chap doors and run away* and *shite alight* both games involved either chapping the door and running off or more daring tying a piece of thread onto the door knocker and going into the back close and pulling at the thread. We always picked a bottom door for quick escape. On occasion we picked Mr Cairney's door, it was madness, he was very good to me, and it was right next door from our house, anyway, we went ahead, I was tugging away at the thread, this is after three answers to the door and we were all laughing in the back close, when suddenly all my friends did a runner and I was pulling the thread, I looked around to the silence and Mr Cairney's son who had a big massive gut grabbed me and started slapping me around the head, he was so angry, what he did was climbed out the back window and came in the back close.

I had no chance of an excuse it was so embarrassing, he dragged me into my door and held me till my mum came to the door, I tried to get in first by stating he had battered me for nothing, my mum listened to Mr Cairney's son and added to the thick ear treatment. My biggest fear was always would my mum tell my oldman, she confirmed she wouldn't and that was the matter settled, however, the trade off was good behaviour for at least the next week, well I would try my hardest.

On reflection the second trick was much more dangerous. We gathered freshly dropped dog shit and rapped it in paper, sat it near a neighbour's door and lit the paper; we then kicked hell out the door hoping the neighbour would open it and stamp on the fire and the shit. Gladly there was no horror stories and we didn't get caught either.

Up stairs was Mrs Rooney, a very nice woman, large grown up family, very experienced in life, she was very fond of my mum and they enjoyed each others company, next door from Mrs Rooney was Shugs brother Michael and his wife Jean, they had two children Linda about 2 years older than me and Thomas, he was the same age, on the top of the close was the Fleming's and the Preston's.

The Fleming's were an older couple and their daughter and her two older sons lived with them. They had a wee corgi dog called Timmy, I remember they had a very nice house, they even painted the white parts of the stairs and landing, they had 3 clothes poles and everybody else borrowed each others. Their front door was varnished and all ours were painted with white gloss, they were the toffs of the close in my opinion.

Next door to them was the Preston's, they had a fairly large family, the dad was called Jackie and the mother was Margaret, they had one son and 4 daughters. That's all I remember them having anyway. Robert was older than me, he hung around with the big team and all his sisters were older than me aswell.

Throughout our 16 years in 32 Willow Street, Temple, there were a few changes to the neighbours. Mr Cairney's family all left and he became ill, he took a massive stroke, it was very sad to see him struggle to achieve the simplest of tasks, Mr Cairney died and a younger family moved into his house. Mrs Rooney

Andy Bell

left; she got a house in Knightswood, the place to be for peace and quiet and much better houses, but never the same levels of community or neighbourhood atmosphere, it was like breaking up a big family. The new next-door neighbours never fitted in, we always got shit from the woman for playing in the close and we hired a skip as a welcoming present and got it dumped in her garden. We also dressed up their wee dog which was just a puppy, we grabbed it into our house, it was like a small Labrador but a Heinz 57 variety, we put a jumper and a string vest on the dog and took it to their door and kicked the door, they must have had a surprise when they opened the door that day. The vest never went to waste the dad fae the house wore the vest playing a football side up a few weeks later.

I do believe your close or street was your world at that younger age, there wasn't a high pressure of material items of furniture or clothing and parents would get by with what they had or they accepted the odd hand me down. Twice a year you got a treat of new clothes, Christmas and the first Sunday in May.

One of my mates *Fajjy* stayed in the next close from us, same side of the street, tap dancer, he used to save up his pocket money for the latest football strip, Scotland or Rangers, Fajjy had two older brothers, no sisters, his dad had a good job, he worked in Barr and Stroud, good payers and they always had a

Christmas party every year for the employers children and grandchildren.

Fajjy was always aloud to take a friend along to this party, the biggest attraction was Santa's present, and this wasn't your traditional selection pack and colour book and pens, Oh No! the very best up to date toys and games, equivalent to having two Christmases, so when this party approached everybody was Fajjy's pal, we all sneaked in with him, falling out and in all the way to the party date, he could blackmail us with the party, I never made the invite but it was something to go for when it came about, apart from that we all got on very well.

Our wee gang was called *the young young scurvy* Gang members were Nosher (me), Skin (my brother), Fajjy, Spud, Tee-M, Fish, Masty, The Tolland's (two brothers) Kingy, Donnie, Gardo, Kenny, big Louie, the Mowits and many others like Scotty, Hammy, Bunnet, Alan Chalmers, Bungo, Bellie, Wee Banjo were from different streets and came and went throughout our growing up, there was the younger team below us, and all the girls aswell. Sandra Ingles, Patricia Lynch, Spike Milligan, Joyce Connolly, Pauline Chalmers and so on. This was only some of the bigger Temple family.

We spent hundreds of hours playing street games, football, two man hunt, kick the can, beds, Big Ben (skipping ropes) and Kirby. We must have spent and average 4 to 6 hours a day growing up playing street games, prior to exploring beyond temple.

Andy Bell

The boys played football morning, noon and night in all weather. Christmas time, new boots, football strips and snow – didn't matter to us, up to the football pitch at Temple primary school, no problem, 5 / 11er's or 10 / 21er's. The big team played on the pitch, so we had to pick and choose when we could use it without any hassle. It was always a major break through when the big team would pick you to play in their side. I remember that feeling when they were picking the teams for the Sunday football from the wall and you are almost last to get picked. When the opposition captain suggests...you have the last remaining three. It makes you feel really unwanted; you just tried harder to prove them wrong for not picking you sooner.

I remember every year both Celtic and Rangers held an open day for their fans, meet the players and kick footballs into the stand, this one year both open days were on the same day, so me and moondog got money from dad to go to parkhead, but most of my pals were going to Ibrox park so we secretly agreed to the Rangers open day, we had to plank our Celtic scarf's and borrowed Rangers scarf's off Fajjy, who agreed to attend the Celtic open day the following year, it was a deal. If we got caught my dad would kill us, so we went to the open day, the old main stand was open, it was free entry, they kicked balls into the stand and paraded their new players, the day passed ok, we told my dad that we had a great day at Celtic park, so that was the end of that day, not so easy! Fajjy a week later came to my door and said

"*I have something to show you, quick into the room*" he had a copy of the Rangers news, he said "*look at the front page*", "*fuck sake I'm fucking deed*" I said, my eyes nearly fell out my head, me and moon, with Rangers scarf's on, giving it big supporter waves 'take ma picture mister look' in a crowd celebrating the open day, it said *Pictures of Rangers rewarding loyal fans at the annual open day*. Well my belly hit the ground and released a trumpet load of farts, my stomach was churning and I felt all weak like I was gonny pass out, someone would see it and tell my dad, it took a few days but we new it would happen and sure as god it did, one of his dart team mates, said to my da, "*John is that not your boys in the Rangers news?*, "*no chance*" he said, then had a closer look, I got battered for it, moon-dog said it was my idea, I also got kept in for a week and for the record, Fajjy has still to attend Parkhead with me.

I must give a special mention to "lucky Didges" middins (bins) before I forget, there is no doubt that within the few streets of Temple where we stayed the bins were poor and nothing lucky about them nobody threw out anything of any value, one day moondog made a bad decision to raid the bins around our backs and ended up getting his nose butt with a dug in the middin. However all was not lost we did have lucky didges near Willow Street the lane next to Bonners the butchers on Fulton Street was good for the luckies, Linden Street the bought houses side and Temple Gardens was rich pickings. I suppose I would best describe a lucky midden as evidence that someone has had a good clear out of their house or someone has kicked the bucket, we became the unofficial beneficiaries of the deed, fur coats and lots of shoes for our ma's and grannies, if we came across a lucky it was a secret location until we had selected from our mates a luckie didgy salvage team, remembering the finder had first crack at the goodies.

On one occasion me and fish found a wee lucky at Temple gardens, we started looking into the bags and discovered lots of nurses uniforms and badges and a bag of nurses watches you could clip onto the uniforms, so we decided we should put the nurses uniforms on and clip the watches to the front of the uniforms, we thought it was so cool to dress up as nurses, but we made the big mistake of walking down Fulton street dressed as nurses trying to flog the watches to make money for swedgers for our big den up the widdy. We got pelters off the women and men and our pals for dressing up like big sissies, we had to put up with the ambulance noises made towards us from our mates for ages, I told fish it was a bad idea, I needed to stop listening to him.

Collecting gingee's

We always had plenty of local workplace options to gather our gingee's; (empty ginger bottles or Glass checks) we always kept our contacts and places to collect a major secret, when to collect, what day/time to collect, what door of the work place to enter. All this information was classified or your income was wiped out, we had to be careful we didn't get followed, if the gingee's were raided when you turned up, it usually caused a local war and big-time fallout, gingee blagger's were classed as modern day cattle rustlers.

Our days where guaranteed full of adventure, building new dens, or finding another work contact that gave us gingees, this was about the only one good reason we broke rank and kept secrets, and one other was the location of a good set of bogey wheels.

Temple always seems to produce the odd chibber, murderer, or crazy family. It's strange that instead of positive community events, what you remember is the notorious side of people, families and incidents. Morton's the bakery, always left the pies; apple turnover's and rolls out to cool. The rolls were amazing, soft and warm when they were just made, we used to sneak into the bakery via the 116 boys brigade hall or just off Crow road beside the doctors, over the fence we'd grab the board full of fresh rolls, by the time you got back down the road the tray was half empty or half full whatever way you look at it. The police could have followed the trail of rolls to find the blaggers. We had to do this after 10pm, if my dad was at the darts I could go on the raid, I would tell my mum a made up story about how I got the rolls from someone I knew.

The local cops didn't have to chase us, they new who we were; they identified us from a mile away. If they did catch us playing football in the street or if we were making a lot of noise; it was in the book on pencil that meant we got a warning. A well known local cop, a stout sergeant, he would never chase you as he knew were everybody stayed and he used to first threaten you with your mum or dad. When we got booked my brother used to insist on giving them his full title. The police would line us all up for playing football or shouting out at them at a distance. Then ask our names, everybody gave straightforward answers, and then it came to my brother John. *"Name?* The big polis would ask, *"John Aloysius Jude Bell"*. The young cop would stare at him and say, *"spell Aloysius"* that's when the fun began, he couldn't spell Aloysius, but he would answer by suggesting the cop asks his big brother, then the crowd would all start trying to convince the cop that this was his proper name, but none of us could spell it.

When new rookie cops arrived in the area, they had a name to make for themselves. They were pests as far as the last letter of the law was implemented, they didn't know how to approach the young team to build relations, they lacked experience and didn't exercise any flexibility or warning, they wanted charges under their hat and to keep in line with the sergeant. This often happened and led too difficult situations. I remember a new rookie called *half-pint;* he was very aggressive in his approach he was given a hard time by most of the young team in the Temple area. He used to pick on individuals, always giving them lots of hassle, he was verbally abused continuously, but that's all it took to turn the reasonable relationship we had with the local cops into a tense and serious situation, plus the old sergeant was off the scene by this time, old style beat cop went out the door to make way for a new arrogant, less practical approaches applied to policing by the new rookies, including real issues around the lack of basic communication skills.

Boundaries

Temple as mentioned was situated in the north west of Glasgow, it boundered Bearsden, Knightswood, and Anniesland, it's population depended where you set the boundaries, we tended to live in upper Temple which was set between Temple police station traffic lights and down Fulton street to the old bridge at the signal box bar. (The siggy)

Before you reach the Bowie, beyond the bridge, was lower Temple that was its length and breadth, one side of the street, not the pub side but the housing side included, Hemlock Street, Willow street, Succoth street, Linden street, Rosewood street, Greywood street etc. The breadth went down past Glencoe Street and stopped prior to reaching great Western road, probably not going through the lane at the old builder's yard / coalery.

There were always plenty of factories in the area and most of the local families had someone or numbers of one family working in the factories. The gang fae woodhouse street used to make tape dens, they turned out like igloos blended into a tree or bushes along the old railway, our dens were in the widdy (wood-yard) up in the rafters, you could acquire all the wood you wanted, we also made dens in other areas out with Temple, we had really good dens behind the picture hall at Anniesland (the Odeon) it was a wild overgrown area, like a jungle.

If Your Feet Are Tired And Weary

We had many adventures down there. Temple itself had many characters with their own street corners to stand at.

The *'two bob mob'* who were all mixed ages, red noses, rubbing their hands together, shuffling their feet around on the same spot, always saying *'hello'* to all passers by. One of the corner mob was wee John Mullmo, sadly he passed away recently, what a guy, every time we passed John he would shake your hand, *"how's it gaun wee Bell?* Or *"how's it gaun young Nosh?* All these guys new your dad and were always keen to give you a line of advice, all street based philosophers in their own right. I always wondered why they didn't work and always stood at the corner sharing drink, swigging out of a bottle in all types of weather. We found the odd one unconscious, pure blootered, we thought they were dead; they just drank till they dropped and in most cases cracked their head on the pavement or wall. We used to get a laugh from the corner mob, we used to walk past them in a line rubbing our hands and shuffling, the brave ones put an empty wine bottle up to their mouth and joked he was steamin' staggering past, they took this in good spirit most of the time.

Temple was like a massive family, everybody knew everybody, and most families all had relations in and around the area. The community was made up of wee mammies, grannies, who had tartan shopping trolleys and da's returning home dirty from their day's

Andy Bell

work, partial to a wee drink at the weekends, even the older people in the area were highly respected by everybody, very rarely did you hear of muggings or house breakings in the area. There would be nowhere to hide if you did this to your *ain folk* even things like stealing motors, it just didn't happen. Fajjy's dad had a wee mini; every night he took his battery up the stairs with him, just to be safe, not everybody's dad had a motor, we had a car, my dad always got the works land rover home at night and weekends, it was his, he would tell us he was the boss and no-one else used it.

Glasgow Fair

I always remembered the Glasgow fair, holiday time for the working class, were all the main factories closed for two weeks and all the dads got two weeks holiday money on top of their wages, it was unbelievable, everybody was happy, my dad used to finish for his holidays, sometimes he would work the holidays if we were not going on holiday, but what was special about Glasgow Fair, everybody in the family would get a good bung off my dad and his workmates if they came home with him. My mum would get chocolates; everyone got a treat, a full supper of choice for everyone. I would go for the chicken supper; it was a must, ginger and sweets aswell. That was the first time I saw a fifty-pound note, nobody would believe me. My dad even let me hold it. There were six of them. I remember thinking I could buy a full lorry of alpine ginger and all my mates a chicken supper, I wouldn't have to ask for chipped fruit, I could buy what I wanted. My dad let me show my mates a fifty pound note at the door, he got fed up when I kept asking him to show people, four times the door went, my dad had enough, for that one day I thought we were the richest family in Temple, if only for that day, it was amazing!

I always got a larger bung fae my dad because I was the oldest, he would give me two quid. I had lots of pals on these occasions, I used to take out a pound and buy lots of ginger and sweets, but eventually I had a sore belly, that's when my dad got angry with me. "*How much have you got left?* This was two hours after I was given the two pounds. "*I've got a pound left, but I've gave my mum the rest to save up*" "*Get out my sight" he* would growl, all my mates were off celebrating someone else's rich tidings. My belly was sore, a full bottle of ginger and chocolate, a full chicken supper; I was ready for my bed. I had blown it another year I'll be more careful with my big bung next year I would say to myself.

My brother got one pound fifty and still had it, he now had more than me and no sore belly to match, he was keeping his money till mine was finished, he'd drink some of my ginger and I would give him half a mars bar, I would try to talk him into putting our monies together for Saturday to go to the swimming but he didn't agree, we'd end up fighting because he would try and annoy me with his money, I would call him *'banana dick'* and attack him. We always had a good fight, but he took flakies, he would lift things and throw them. I remember once I ate his selection pack at Christmas as he over slept and he trapped me between the single beds and punched into my face. This was early hours of Christmas morning. I spent Christmas day with two big black eyes; my dad thought it was funny he would say *"it deserves you right greedy arse"*

Oh! Mammy! Daddy!

I remember the time my brother went missing, it was pure panic throughout Willow street, what really sparked off the real panic was a neighbour claiming to have seen him heading towards the canal himself, the last sighting from my mum was around 4pm and this was about 9pm. I could see my mum and dad starting to be really worried, I heard my mum at one point saying *"oh please god not again"* thinking the very worse had happened. No one else could confirm the canal sighting of John. I remember I was outside chapping all his mates doors checking out all the possible dens, there was no sign of him. I started to panic, I was standing in the close and my mates were all asking me how I was feeling and I was crying saying *"he's my wee brother!* Although we were always fighting I would have clearly missed him.

I remember one of the lassies saying *"children get white coffins, lovely so they are"* I started crying uncontrollably attempting to have conversation and cry at the same time, what a mess I was in, under normal circumstances the neighbours would have cleared us out the close for the noise, but this was one exception. The police finally became involved, and they promptly interviewed the wee woman who sighted John heading towards the nolly. The police organised two frog divers and lighting etc, when I heard this update not from my parents but through the street news flashes or gossip mongers the statements became explicit "*that wee boy Bell has drowned in the nolly and the frog men are trying to find his body*" I was crying my hardest and saying out loud "*oh mammy daddy please god please god!* The crowd thought I was going daft. I needed an adult preferably my mum or dad to comfort me and tell me that everything would be all right, but it didn't happen.

My parents were having their own grief in the house, my dad headed back up the nolly and my mum was surrounded by neighbours, talking, making tea, reassuring my mum everything would be alright.

Then around 10pm a breakthrough, Mrs. Rooney asked my mum if she had checked the whole house, my mother said she had, but she decided to re-check and in the end room we had a old dossy bed, it had two mattresses, it was great for jumping off the wardrobe, bang your head on the ceiling, Mrs Rooney heard snoring noises and low and behold between both mattresses soaking wet with sweat '*banana dick*', why or how he was there has never been answered, but John got woke up and my dad and mum were so embarrassed they had to explain this find to the police and I gave him a slap for making me cry like a fudd in front of everybody in the street, but deep down we were all glad he was still with us. My dad decided to get rid of the old bed and mattress.

The Nolly

Our association with the nolly goes back years, we had the canal running from Kirkintilloch right down to Dumbarton, but we mainly travelled as far as Maryhill in one direction and Westerton station at the most in the other direction. We loved the canal, even with it's dangers, winter it was iced over and summer it was great for swimming, it had many loch gates between Temple, two bridges, we used to swim mainly at 'old Alex's house' just up from the Temple road bridge. We used to get changed at the orange halls across from the main loch gate; it was a suntrap crossing the road bare feet, small stones causing jaggy discomfort. We used to spend a lot of time discussing who was 'breaking the ice' who was in first or organising a group entry, but when you jumped in the rest of the gang were still standing on the bank. Old Alex had a plum tree around his back, it was good for a raid, but old Alex was good to the young team, he used to blow up inside tubing's from tyres for us to use in the nolly, we always were told that the weeds under the water could pull us under so every time your feet felt weeds we would quietly panic.

We spent at times most of our summer holidays in the nolly, swimming right along the nolly bank, the other gangs from Temple had their nolly swimming patch, the Bowie swam up to the white bridge at Westerton.

Andy Bell

We tended to stay at our bit, at the back of your mind always lay the dangers of when you dive in are you going to hit a car, a washing machine or any other dodgy objects because it was an unofficial dumping ground, clearly with many dangers. When it came to the nolly I would have considered myself as a bit of a 'shitbag'. I hardly ever did the big unknown dives off the loch gate, the big ones or swim the nolly lengths that involved swimming from one loch gate to another with no side exit until you reached the other loch gate because right up the both sides, it was six foot wide, both sides of weeds. I know you had to swim right up the centre to avoid the dreaded weeds. My mate Fish was one of the gang who did the nolly lengths the canal produced local hero's, for swimming, diving the high loch gate and even the Temple bridge. John did the Temple motor bridge right down the nolly sides were concrete because it was underneath and part of the large red motor bridge one of the big team offered John aka skin a half a mars bar if he would do the bridge, he accepted the challenge to my amazement. He was never a good swimmer and hadn't long learned to swim, I pleaded with him not to do it privately, but the delighted audience talked him into it. This was one part of the nolly that was not tried and tested to check if there was any objects, but he didn't care he was going for it. The dive involved going up onto the busy road climbing onto the bridge and going for it, he was advised by the 'big team' who were posting the prize to try and keep to the middle of the water.

If Your Feet Are Tired And Weary

It was 'oh! mammy, daddy oh please god' time for me again, quietly this time because I would have got the blame if this had went wrong, his diving position was similar to both hands clasped together on his head in the praying position, what a sight, he stood up hobbled on the red bridge, the crowd were all cheering, we had the potential of a hero or a badly injured silly boy, off he went, he missed the concrete edge of the nolly by five feet and emerged from under the water shocked but alive and there was loud cheering. I was going about saying *"do you know what my wee brother did the other day?* The crowd picked him out the water and he was carried down Temple like a real hero.

Another hero of the nolly was 'big Masty' he saved Fajjy's life, they were messing about the canal edge one day on their own and Fajjy slipped in, couldn't swim and Masty managed to get Fajjy out, he was a real hero for that and Mr & Mrs McFarlane definitely gave him a reward and I know Fajjy was very pleased for his courage. I think an adult also became involved in the rescue, Masty was rewarded more credit from our gang for saving Fajjy's life, he never fully joined us but went on the occasional outing and was permitted into the odd den, and his personal bullying was reduced. Some of the lassies used to come up the nolly, they were older and had grown boobs, I remember the day we grabbed an older lassie and threw her in. she had her swimming bikini on and was messing about the canal bank, *"I might go in"* she would say, all the patter, fed up listening

Andy Bell

to her shite about going in, we grabbed her and gave her a helicopter entrance, spinned her around and when she was leaving the water her bikini was around her waste, we couldn't believe the size of her boobs, they were amazingly big, after that incident everybody wanted to be her boyfriend. We all fancied our chances to get a private viewing of those boobs; she just became another nolly hero.

Dossy Park

We used to leave the nolly and go up to *dossy* that was better known as 'Dawsholm park', that's were we played two man hunt and had a Tarzan swing near the railway line. Dossy was a great park, it was stretched over a large area, it went from the edge of Temple to Maryhill and to the edge of Westerton, it included the pitch and putt, the incinerator, the froggy, squirrels and football pitches, and a massive play park, easy to get lost. We used to play on the Tarzan swing for ages which was a thick rope tied to a tree with a thick log of wood at the bottom for a seat. The pain you received from the seat due to *boardees* was unbelievable, that's were you start off on the swing and two, three or even four people jumped on the swing with you still on it at the bottom of them all, it was very painful in the Kelvin Halls, that was definitely a nut cruncher. We used to fight to boardee the lassies, they used to tell us who could boardee them, I was hardly ever a first choice.

I remember we were warned about the *wolfee* half man, half wolf, we used to run through the park scaring each other, *"there's wolfee run for your life!!* We used to run from the narrow dark paths of the park, one leading to another going around in circles until we reached the open part of the swings, space ships and sand pits. It was safety and you could see Temple from this advantage point.

One big fear of the park was meeting up with the Maryhill fleet or other gangs, they used to hang about the park as well, and it was safe to say we had the park as part of our patch; it was in our control, at least the main swing part.

We use to roll down the hill at the main swing area from the very top right down past the big giant tree at the bottom near Bearsden Road. The competition was who could do the most 'rollies' doon the hill. I think the record was about 160 but it was sore on your heed and it was difficult to stand straight, it made you very dizzy. Dawsholm park also attracted boy Scouts and Guide groups, they used to do the 'pretend' camping, arrive at 12 noon in the park and leave at four in the afternoon, they used to pitch a tent, light a fire and cook food, we used to attack their camp site just for a laugh, running through the area shouting loud and disturbing the scout badge assessments.

The park also housed the incineration, it was massive, and you could see the Dawsholm incinerator chimney from miles away. We used to climb under the fence to look for any 'lucky goodies'.

We went to the end were the public could drive in and dump household goods and general rubbish into big containers. We found bikes, golf clubs, and toys. We had to rip open the black bags and someone had to keep 'the edgy' for the watchy, he had a wee hut at the front gate. There was also a house attached to the incinerator. We stopped going to the containers because one of the young team ripped open a black bag and it was full of dead puppies. Smelling, we were frightened incase we found a dead body.

Every park had a parky; we spent lots of hours being chased about the park by the parky in his wee green van. We had to make sure the parky didn't recognise us, he new what we looked like from moving us on. There was a large vet hospital next to the park, it had a giant hay stack in it, we could build dens up there, we got caught once and they marched us up to the main office at the gate, took our names and told us that our dads would receive a bill for the burst hay stacks. The bills would never arrive due to the duff names and addresses, but that stopped us going there.

Within the entrance of Dawsholm park there was a tap, drinking well, we spent many hours soaking wet, the well could spray out water right up to ten feet if you screwed the small drinking part off, then you could press your fingers onto it and direct the water to the rest of the gang. We spent hours doing this. The best laugh at the well was sitting in the bushes beside the well watching young lovers strolling, walking down the paths hand in hand heading towards the water well, parting company briefly for a small drink, retaining eye contact but the well was all set for ten feet of squirting when they leaned over the well for a drink usually the boyfriend saying *"you first darling"* he was offering to turn the handle, then it would rapidly soak the lassie or the guys face, hair

Andy Bell

and jumper right up the nose it would go, we rolled about the bushes laughing.

Another favourite at the well was lying on the ground beside the well then someone would turn the well on and your task was to catch as much water in your mouth as possible, it went straight up in the air and looped down to the ground. We had to stay on the ground adjusting slightly to were the water was landing, people who chickened out of things usually got 'itches' put down their backs 'Itches' where big red/orange seeded things that made you itch for ages, most of the time everybody did the 'dare'.

Truth, derr, double derr, promise or command

We used to play truth, derr, double derr, promise or command the game consisted of one person setting a dare for another and so on and you had to do it, that game was painful and risky, climbing high trees, running up to complete strangers and saying bad things, trousers at ankles across the main park or hanging from a tree, it was mostly enjoyable when the lassies agreed to play it. I always chose derrs because it was risky and mad. The 'double derrs' where always boring. We usually imposed a boundary on derrs like sending someone to Anniesland cross was not on, you had to do it within the park, a few people worked hand in hand; a lot of derrs were requests for private views of someone's downstairs for example; "*I dare you to show one of the lassies your mortis lock (cock) in the bushes*", and you couldn't come out until she saw it proper. It would require the lassie to shout "*I can see it*" sometimes you could make a deal with the lassie just to say she had seen it, or if she had already saw it anyway we could just suggest there had been no change to your wully since the last viewing. Showing your pants, bum and sheriff's badge or balloon knot was amongst the most common requests.

Andy Bell

The park bordered Maryhill so you had to watch how deep you travelled towards Maryhill, we never hung about the park alone or later at night we mainly travelled in packs or small street teams stuck together, or teamed up with other people from wider Temple, especially around the summer time and swimming in the nolly.

Jacques Cousteau

Jacques-Yves Cousteau was the "scuba man of the 70s" he has been referred to as the *"explorer of the world of silence".* He invented scuba and pioneered unaided deep sea diving and underwater photography. I would like to claim me and moondog on one memorable occasion used his underwater techniques indoors in the middle of Temple not even in the nolly. However we never reached stage two of our basic training.

Around 1970 the Glasgow Corporation (the council) were to make a decision to demolish (upper Temple), our houses and most of the older tenement buildings around us including Willow street, Hemlock street, Succoth street, part of the top of Fulton street and Succoth road. All the gang was clearly devastated at the decision but the parents were tempted by a possible better house and a one off disturbance payment. The Corporations excuse was the buildings were sinking. It's always strange to discover they planned and did eventually build fancy private houses with back and front doors on the "sinking land" including army accommodation. Social engineering without a doubt I understand regeneration and renewal but this was a profit driven decision the start of a planned corporation strategy to change the social status of Temple from a "area of priority treatment" (APT) and of course it was close to Bearsden and the emerging trendy west end.

Andy Bell

So what this meant was the beginning of the end of our wonderful place we called home, full of magical people, real characters' and great memories both happy and sad, the whole community were gutted by the decision to demolish Temple.

Over the next 5 years from 1970 the corporation started to stage manage the re-location of many families, most of whom wanted to remain within the Temple area, but the reality was they could not offer Temple to most due to the lack of houses remaining in the area. I remember each time a family would accept a house offer and get a date to move, then on the day of the removal it was like suffering a bereavement in the family, with everybody watching the removal van as if it was a funeral motor, wondering, who's next to go.

Luckily for us we were nearly last on the timescale for demolition, so they started clearing Hemlock street, house by house, close by close, with all the families rightly holding out for the right house offer, I think you got offered 3 or 4 offers with each offer slightly improving, it was easy to spot the ongoing disputes between the remaining tenants and the housing, last up the close, left in isolation for 3 to 6 months with all the buildings around you getting knocked down. All this activity created a great opportunity for us to play with all the empty houses the biggest play park in the world we could own a close each and if brave enough claim a full street. I remember bon-fire night we had hundreds of doors from the houses, the technique was simple to get a door off we stuck a hammer at the hinge and fold the door back, off in seconds. Doors also became very valuable for den making single or double decks; some dens were real fancy with carpets left behind in the hooses there were always many dens on the go with each den having *owners* usually the builders and door collector helpers had earned the right to hang about the den then invited guests, lassies and people hanging about outside desperate to get inside, this was usually the young young team. Then the disputes would arrive whose den was best or stolen ideas, this would ultimately lead to burning down dens to settle scores and differences.

We became the unofficial demolition squad for the corporation; we also stripped out all the scrap including lead tanks in the loft, copper boilers, all the lead and copper piping throughout the building and not forgetting the lead on the roof. We had all the escapes planned out when we got the edgy for the police or security.

I did feel rotten for the last house left in the close; we still went ahead and blagged their tank from the loft, when they were at work. We had a method of kicking through the plaster into the top floor houses (not occupied) we never broke into anybody's house we had principals and standards within reason. We searched the lofts for any luckies left behind; the lofts were minging big time with everybody's crap left behind. If you were on loft duty you were pure black by the end of the day.

One day me and moondog came across 2 old war gas masks with the filters attached they were in good nick, so we decided to keep them and take them home, it was a Sunday because it was bath night in the Bell house, what a task bathing 6 weans with only enough hot water for one bath, so we took it in turns each week to see who gets in the bath first the boys or lassies, lucky for us it was our turn first, so me and moondog got into the bathroom with our top of the range deep sea diving masks, one each.

I remember the French guy Jacques-Yves Cousteau was on the telly, swimming under water beside all the fish, so we both thought we were yer man aswell as underwater treasure hunters.

We put our masks on and agreed an underwater communication system with the thumbs-up and down for diving, it was great fun, even putting marbles in the bath and hunting for them, we tried talking to each other under the water. The bath was half-full when we started and not the warmest; we started taking turns diving into the bath, the water was everywhere, we didn't bother getting washed we were having such a good time, being treasure hunters. It was amazing!

Then from out of the blue, a loud bang on the door, my mum had been listening to see what we were up too, we were already over our time, she shouted *"what are you two up to? open this door"*, our masks were all steamed up and we panicked we couldn't reply only a muffled sound, she shouted to my dad *"John, they perr a cunts are up to nae good, not getting washed, they wont open the door",* we both jumped out the bath grabbed the big towel we were going to share for getting dried, my dad was at the door shouting, "*open this door, or the perr of ye are getting a sore arse".* I turned and looked into the bath it was pure black in color with six inches of water and a black ring around the bath were the water levels started, I stared at John and he stared at the bath, shit! We're in big trouble. I opened the door, we both stood with our gas masks on and holding the towel at our waist, my dad had a stunned look about him, he took one look at the water, grabbed us both, slapped our ears and kicked our arses along the hall we were still wearing our masks and told to go straight to bed.

We decided to get rid of our diving equipment. The next day we gave up our gas masks and new found hobby as treasure hunters as it caused us too much bother. I guess my dad must have had a laugh at his work whilst describing the diver's scene to his work mates. I think we even had a laugh ourselves looking back, I know the story brought many tears of laughter to my workmates many years on whilst reminiscing at lunch breaks.

Andy Bell

Temple Primary School, Spencer Street, 1970s. The school was designed by Henry Higgins in 1899 for the New Kilpatrick School Board and featured a distinctive wooden bell turret.

The cyro cellotape factory Succoth Road

If Your Feet Are Tired And Weary

Annies the chip fruit shop, Fulton Street

Posh hooses Anniesland

Andy Bell

Sloan's dairy the tick shop, Fulton Street

Me (age 4) with auntie molly's lassies

If Your Feet Are Tired And Weary

St Ninians primary (second row from top, centre, wearing my famous horses' shirt)

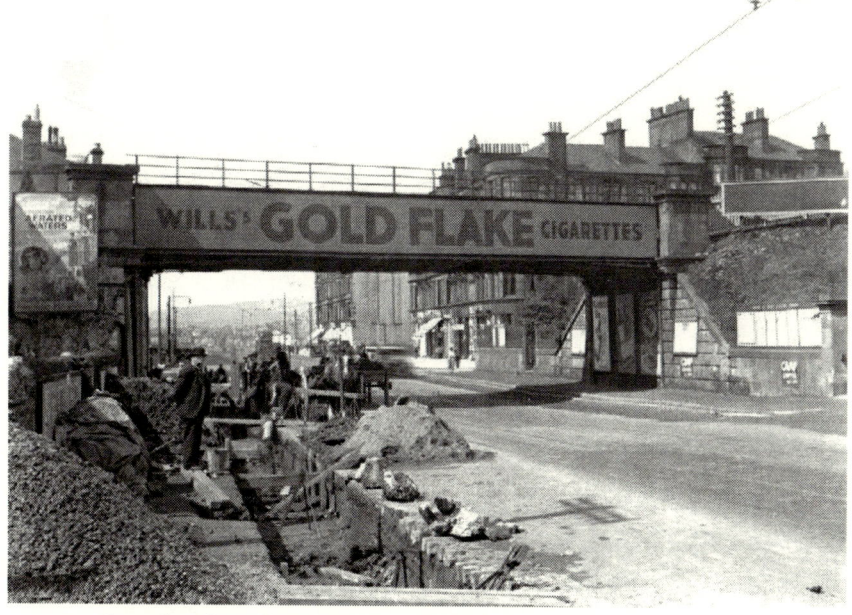

Anniesland Railway Bridge at station

Hacked off

We used to save up all our scrap lead, copper boilers, our system was straight forward we had a plank or stash for the scrap which was an old coal bunker in a close or planked it inside an empty hoose. When we had collected enough swag for a run to the scrappy, the scrappy of our choice was always the yellow house next to the Kelvin hall, the old guy that ran the yard was a bit dooteray, we would wrap half bricks into the lead and put it through for the weight, he used to ask us to throw the scrap in a big pile once he weighed it, but we used to pass it back onto our pile for a double weigh-in.

One day we sent moondog down to Anniesland cross taxi rank to grab a black hack and bring the taxi up to Temple to load up the scrap, we had to keep the edgy (lookout) for the police and move fairly fast. On this occasion the swag was in our old coal bunker inside the close, so we proceeded to fill the taxi, after two or three trips in and out the close we heard a door slam and ran out onto the street to discover the hackney fucker had done a runner with our scrap. We spent weeks looking for the driver, the scrap was between six of us, so if we ever caught the guy he would have suffered along with his taxi.

It meant we had to do some overtime to make up for our loss, when we got a hack in the future we kept one of the young team in the back at all times whilst we loaded the cab.

The Night auld Dixie came to town?

It was shaping up to be another fun packed weekend living in Temple, what was the big adventure this weekend, who knows? Straight across the road from my hoose in the street, a young blonde good looking woman stayed in the bottom hoose. I don't think she had a man living with her and she hadn't lived there very long. I noticed a few times in the week a fancy Datsun motor, real flash, it was parked outside her close. I caught a flashing glimpse a few times of a guy smart dressed with the 70s wet tight perm look and sporting a thick black moustache, he went into the big blondes house and left a few hours later. I thought to myself *'this guy is familiar to me, I think I know him'* but wasn't 100% sure where or when or who he was, on the Sunday morning I was at Martins the local paper shop, getting ma dad's usual, Sunday mail and a bottle of Garvies dark cola and as I walked into the street at my close the big flash motor pulled up in front of me and then the penny dropped, it was fucken Dixie Deans the Celtic man! I was sure of it, (well sort off) as clear as cheap cellotape, my heart skipped a beat, I couldn't believe it, my eyes were seeing things, how fucken cool is that, Dixie Deans super star in Temple, in my street, now our fuckin neighbour, I thought to myself we must mark this very special occasion.

So I dropped off the paper and ginger tae the hoose, grabbed my Celtic scarf and went to gather all

If Your Feet Are Tired And Weary

my pals especially the Celtic supporters, one by one I went around their doors telling them the amazing news, we had a famous guy in our street, they all collected their flags and scarf's. I suggested we give him a big Temple welcome and sing outside the front bedroom window, I managed to get eight mates, it was near lunch time on the Sunday and we started the chanting and waving the flags and scarfs "*Dixie, Dixie, superstar, Dixie, superstar*" after about 2 minutes of us giving our best singing the bedroom curtain moved ever slightly, then I changed the song to, "*Dixie, Dixie geez a wave, Dixie, geez a wave*", no response, then my Rangers supporter pals started arriving, with their flags and scarfs and started singing a song about him being a women, wearing a bra and putting the ball over the bar. Before we knew it, we were trying to out sing each other, we had a good crowd by this time, twenty plus in the women's front garden, then the women came out from the close looking a wee bit upset and said to us "*if you arse holes don't get out my garden, go away and stop that singing I will call the police, there's nae bloody superstar in my house*" (taxi for a couple of fannies moment)

So the outcome of this story is we were young soap dodgers hanging on to the possibility there was a real football hero on our patch, who knows? I do now apologise to the Mr. Dean look alike and being very young we didn't understand you were probably on *fiddlers' elbow duty*, very soon afterwards the fancy car stopped coming to the street, maybe he just thought we were all bad singers.

Buzzing

In the early 70s and into the late 80s snu-gliffing (glue sniffing) or buzzing had arrived onto the scene. The big team were all sniffing well before any of us knew much about it. I don't know how it arrived in Temple, but it had, and also spread through out Glasgow into all the different areas, street by street. I first became aware of buzzing when a guy older than us from Temple hanged himself from an old railway bridge near the Bowie.

I remember going down to the spot were the guy hanged himself with my mates, everybody was talking about it, he was sniffing glue prior to committing suicide, we all just stood staring at the spot wondering *what it was like? What did he look like? Who found him*? all the kind of details you think you need to know so you can go into school the next day and spin the story that you saw the guy hanging and what he was like, sad, but true as an insensitive young guy seeking the attention from your peers.

I do remember the time we discovered the big team were into the glue, it was during the start of a long school summer break when one of my mates followed his big brother with a couple of his pals heading down the back of Anniesland cross up towards the gas works, my pal stayed well back, he witnessed them pouring glue into milk bottles and started sniffing via there noses, they were all laughing and rolling about, my mate was eventually caught spying and warned not to grass or else, he just sat nearby and observed his first glue sniffing experience.

He came to us with his discovery and information and before we knew it we were preparing and organising to try our first buzzing session. We had blagged a half pint of evo stick from a DIY store and got our milk bottles, there was five of us all agreeing to give it a try.

That was the start of a period of real madness, a time that would stretch all our relationships with our parents and get most of us into different levels of trouble, even the lassies were buzzing with us, I suppose it took more of a grip of us because we had just started our summer school holidays and it wasn't unusual to disappear for most of the day without or parents worrying too much about us, after you got your breakfast or even a 20/1 shot with jam and butter (a big outsider) we were off for the day until tea time.

The first time we organised to go buzzing we went to dossy park heading straight for the deep bushes, not even caring about getting attacked by the legendary wolf-man, an old myth of a hairy man that supposedly lived in the park and would randomly attack kids who stray off the parks pathways. (Temple's big foot) The other real danger was bumping into a team from Maryhill; especially if we were not team handed, so armed with our glue and bottles we all gave ourselves small pours into the bottom of the milk bottles and up to our noses we were buzzing away. I think we were more excited than scared we knew we had to avoid getting glue on our hands, face or clothes.

When I started sniffing from the bottle it only took minutes to start to hear the buzzing sound and start to feel very funny inside and outside your body, everything around me slowed down and voices became muffled, nobody was saying much, I started seeing grass growing from my pals heed and thought is was weird looking, a real mix of being freaked out and then laughing about nothing important or all that funny, then one of my mates started crying for a dog of his that died years ago, we were all breaking our ribs laughing because he was bubbling like a fanny for nothing, another pal fell asleep and his hair was all sticking up when he woke up, we all thought this was hilarious. I think you reach a point were you seem not to be in control of your body and everything is in slow motion mode, I think we gave our first experience the thumbs up and it gave us all plenty to talk about with the rest of the team.

The truth is I don't think we considered any of the many dangers surrounding sniffing the glue; it was a great feeling at the time. Another major danger for a lot of the Temple troops was the railways surrounding the whole area, we always crossed the railway line as a short cut to Anniesland and up to dossy park, we even had a tree swing that swung over the railway line. Another important area about buzzing was getting breathalysers after sniffing, due to the smell of glue

If Your Feet Are Tired And Weary

from your breath, I used polo mints, tooth paste, a full mars bar in the gub before going in the house, the front door test, I used to suck in rather than blow out when asked to have my breath smelt, another breathalyser was Tunes, Trebor mints, Victory V's the most smelliest tasting sweets in the world and finally drinking curry sauce from a tray all to avoid detection of glue sniffing.

Trying to avoid face to face contact with your parents was hard, heading straight to your room, shouting *"I'm tired and going to my bed"*. At an early stage we weren't under much suspicion, nobody had been caught as yet; and anyway the parents would always blame each others weans for being a bad influence. I remember we had den's everywhere, we always had somewhere we could go and hang about, they included old empty buildings, the widdy and of course door dens, the guy's fae Woodhouse street used to build tape dens in the old railway they were amazing, and very warm, they blagged the tape from the ciro works, big industrial rolls.

An older guy from Sutcliffe Street was hanging about with us, it worked out he had experience sniffing glue, his sister had big massive bazookas, she used to show us them if we promised not to grab them, it was always hard to resist, she was older than us, she was great for a game of truth derr. I was led to believe she had a huge furry burger, I never saw it, but my pals pulled her bikini bottoms down when they were up the nolly and reported she had indeed a big hairy one. Her brother hung about with us in return for him buying the glue because he was old enough to get served at the shops we gave him a pour. The shops were getting tougher on who they were selling it to, it didn't affect us much we blagged most of ours, they did start putting it behind the counter, by this point everyone knew glue sniffing was becoming a problem in the area. This older guy had a specialty, he could make a 'Goldie' by slowly turning his bottle around with a fresh pour he would coat all the inside of the bottle creating a Goldie, providing the best buzz available, a small DIY shop at the top of Crow road, sold tubes and half pints they used to give you a small red plastic evo stick spreader with your purchase so we all kept them as a membership of the young scurvy buzzers club.

I remember some of my mates going camping to Millport taking with them a tartan shopping trolley full of empty milk bottles, they were warned that milk bottles were very rare on the island; we were spoiled for bottles due to Sloans dairy being in Temple.

It is strange that a lot of the glue sniffing from England and other parts of Glasgow was buzzed from bags into the mouth. We all thought this was minging and didn't entertain this method. Another tell-tale sign and starting to be a problem for us was we were developing ridges across our noses, marks left from pressing the bottles into our faces, lots more spots and spending too much time in our bedrooms. A good pour could last most of the day, stash it and stir it up for a wee buzz at night, some of my mates started buzzing more frequently, we all loved playing football but even that was suffering, everybody was too busy buzzing. I remember having a good pour planked from one of my sessions the night before, so I decided in the morning to head up to the widdy and got my pour from my plank freshened it up and went into Temple primary school shed at the back of the school and started buzzing myself, never again!!!! I looked up and saw the school crumbling down brick by brick, it was an old fashioned brick building, it looked as clear as anything, I smashed my pour on the ground and started screaming like a mad-man, shouting at the top of my voice *"the fucking schools falling down"* I ran from the school grounds, bolted across Fulton street, not even noticing the cars, not even hearing the drivers honking their horns at me, I was just so convinced the school was crumbling to the ground, I headed into a close and tried to calm down, I popped my head out the close and with a sigh of relief and total confusion the school was still standing, I shat myself big time that morning.

One of my pal's big brothers caught him sniffing and grassed him to his dad, this was the start of a lot of trouble for all of us, we were now all under the microscope, all the parents placing 'keep away' orders on my mates' cause they got grassed or captured. One of the parents was so mad she was going around the doors warning the other parents about the glue sniffing, I was lucky my dad was at work when she chapped our door *"Chrissie I'm just warning you, they are all at it"* I just told my mum the guys big brother made him do it and we didn't hang about with glue sniffers. My mum believed me.

Due to me being the oldest sibling in my family, I had no big brothers threatening to kick the shit out of me, however, my mates that got caught buzzing were told by their big brothers that they would batter all their mates caught sniffing with them, so we started having to buzz well away from Temple. It was becoming more difficult to buy or blag glue, the parents via the police wanted the source stopped and warned older adults buying it that they would be severally dealt with. I was clear I didn't want caught with my old man he would kill me.

Glue sniffing was becoming a high risk and unpopular activity, we're 7 months down the line and some of my pals have started getting caught or grassed by big brothers plus mum's and dad's getting confessions from their sons and daughters, naming names to try and save there own arses, at its peak a lot of the guys I new were buzzing at different levels, it was getting a bit crazy, some of my mates were staying out later, even all nighters, 2 of them had ran away due to getting caught sniffing and dogging school and a couple of them got put into young offenders for police assault rather than getting caught, trying to fight their way to freedom. In Temple it was hard with the police because they new who we all were and they didn't have to chase many of us.

If Your Feet Are Tired And Weary

Time was closing in on me and I didn't even know it, not that I cared, I was buzzed out my face, someone broke into a warehouse and stole six gallons of evo stick in big green industrial tins, he sold four and kept two gallons for the troops, amazing, we could get as many pours as we wanted until some arsehole told a school mate from the Bowie were our stash of glue was and that was the end to that, we couldn't prove anything so everybody blamed everybody else.

Some of my mates were dogging school and this brought more crap to their doors when the school board appeared, they spent their day sniffing glue and blagging grub from the shops, you could also buy chipped fruit from 'Annies' on Fulton street, a big bag of soft fruit for 5 or10p always a favourite when going to our many dens.

The eventual night had arrived when I was caught, it was my worst nightmare, it was a Wednesday a very cold winter's night. We had all planned to attend the Scotland game at Hampden Park. I managed to get a pour of glue prior to going to the game and took it all the way to the game hidden inside my snorkel jacket. I was in the old Rangers end I don't even remember who Scotland played the score or nothing about the game, I was sniffing away at the game and we were all buzzing away on the train on the way home.

I kept saying to myself I would plank the pour as I was getting closer to the house, I was well gone, buzzed out my heed, I remember getting to the street and planning to plank my pour around the back behind the drain pipe, but noticed my dad still wasn't in he was still at the darts. I had never been this close to the hoose with glue before; I was just about to make a massive mistake by deciding to sneak the glue into the hoose and into my bedroom which I shared with moondog. It was a quarter bottle pour, I stuck my head into the living room and said to my mum I was off to bed, moondog was already sleeping I opened the window to let out the fumes and started to buzz away in my bed, it wasn't long until my dad came in, he asked my sister Brenda to close our room window as it was getting bitter cold outside, my sister opened our room door and shouted "*dad there's a funny smell in the boys room*" I had put the pour down as I heard my dad coming into the room and he knew right away the smell was glue, me and moondog had two single beds, so right away my dad went over to his bed and grabbed him and smelt his breath, only camel shit from sleeping, he then turned to me and shouted "*It's you ya bastard! you've been sniffing glue*" I was away with it, totally buzzed, "*get out that fucking bed*" my mum had arrived in the room and tried to calm him down, he said "*get ready your going to the police, where's the fucken glue?*' He got the glue from under the bed, somehow, I got my gear on, it was all a blur.

I must have started coming around and remember I started crying, "*I'm sorry, I'm sorry dad I found the glue and just tried it*" he was raging "*move your fucking arse*" he yelled and grabbed me by the scruff of the neck and frog-marched me up to Temple police

If Your Feet Are Tired And Weary

station, my dad had the glue bottle in his other Hand, he just kept saying, "*move your fucking arse*", I had slashed my breeks (peed myself) at the top of our street, having been dragged all the way up Fulton street and the louder I would cry the more slaps and punches I would get on the back of the heed.

We eventually reached the outside of the station, my dad marched straight through the doors slamming them against the wall, still holding onto the scruff of my jumper, at the desk my dad slammed the glue bottle on the counter and said *"I want to know who the fuck is selling them the glue, I have just found this bastard in the hoose sniffing this"* pointing to the bottle, it had all smashed, but the glass was held together with the glue, the Police tried to calm my dad down, *"Calm doon fuck all, you'd better keep this bastard here tonight or I will fucken kill him"* the Police agreed to hold me in a detention room until morning. I was just 15 years old at the time and stuck to my story when the police asked were and who had bought it for me. I told them I was playing football at the school and I saw a big guy plank something behind the fence at the widdy and when I looked it was the glue, I had heard funny stories about it so decided to try it. The next morning my mum came to the police station and took me straight to Dr Adams at the top of Crow Road to seek reassurance I was not hooked on the glue. I told the Dr the same story that I just tried it for the first time, my mum said she was so disappointed with me and that my dad didn't want to see me, I was to go to school and then go straight into my room and stay there including dinner time, I was to eat alone in my room. This isolation and grounding lasted six months, some of this time was self imposed. I was so ashamed, totally gutted I had let my parents down, my mum used to let me watch the odd programme before my dad came in, I suppose in a way I was glad to be in the room due to my feeling of personal disappointment and shame.

I still spoke to my mates at the room window, I even took on a derr one night to run to the bottom of the street in the buff for a full bottle of alpine cola, we used to call it 'sore belly ginger' 12p a litre bottle, I was still grounded, if my dad drove into the street I would have been a gonner, in a way I was glad the glue sniffing had ended for me because some of my mates were still getting into serious shit, I was just looking forward to getting back to football and more innocent adventures away from the dangers of buzzing the glue.

From Big Shaggy to Stan laurel

I remember one day I was walking along the nolley coming from Firhill to Temple with big shaggy Bell (no relation) and Pauline Chalmers the niece of Stevie Chalmers of the 1967 Celtic European cup team. Pauline's parents hated her hanging about Temple they lived across from Knightswood bus garage on Great Western road, top floor in the sandstone houses, she was a right tom-boy, whist walking along the nolley three bigger guy's (men) walked passed us, we were close to Maryhill, they were sniffing glue, they walked passed and asked us for the time, none of us had a watch and replied, *"sorry big man don't know"*, I smelt trouble, big Shaggy was nearly six foot and a full head of hair, all curly, side boxers at 13, he was not known as a fighter but had a giant haystacks look about him.

The next thing we know the three idiots came round the bend charging at us, shouting *"Maryhill fleeto ya bastards come on"* they had bottles in their hands, we all started running, and with Pauline looking like a guy they were into us all, then big Shaggy just stopped and let out a big growl and screamed, *"Temple scurvy come on ya fuckers"* we were still running, we stopped and went back and within a minute we found big Shaggy in the canal, we pulled him out, they had smashed two bottles over his heed, one was a glue bottle, so his hair was all glue and glass, *"why did you stop running Shaggy? Ya fucken mad-man"* I asked him, he said *"I dropped my polo mints and said to myself, fuck it"* we had to stop at auld Alex's hoose at Temple (loch 27) Shaggy was upset because his mum would think he was sniffing glue, so we started cutting his hair and all the glue out with sharp glass from a gingy, we had to cut out lots of his curls, he went from looking like Bill Oddie to looking more like Stan Laurel, we sat at the nolley laughing our heads off, trying to reassure big Shaggy it didn't look that bad, we all agreed a story, he told his mum he burnt his hair at a fire and unfortunately still got his ring cracked and grounded for hanging about fires.

Pauline Chalmers used to play football with us a game of world cup, I broke her foot in a tackle at Temple school pitches by accident whilst playing one day we had to carry her around to Great Western Road to her close and do a runner as she was barred from hanging about Temple, she was screaming her heed off.

Any Extras (school)

The Dinnie (dinner school) and Extra dinners was the highlight of primary school without a doubt (Nosher my nickname I wonder why?), mince and tatties followed by Carmel cake and custard what a treat it was up there with the amazing games of football we had at playtime and lunchtime, we used to play against the classroom next to us throughout primary, down with the coats as goalposts and the game was on, serious business.

My first school, Knightscliffe primary school was burnt to the ground by the Bowie, it was a wee wooden school at the bottom of Fulton street, not much time to settle in, then it was torched, it was just along from Cameron Campbell the VW garage, it had a car wash near it, in the summer we used to walk through the carwash with cars like real daft fannies, pure soaking wet, the guy in the car show room knew we were a wee bit mental, he used give us car posters in return for not touching his cars. After the school got burnt down we got bussed in single deckers every day from the top of Fulton Street to Corpus Christie a primary school in Knightswood, the two buses used to race to see who arrived first.

It was a fairly new school we stayed there for over a year and eventually got a more permanent move to St Ninians near the Lincoln boozers on Great Western road. We used to catch the bus at Anniesland either

Andy Bell

a 16 or 33 along to school, the bus took us all the way to the terminus right behind the school, I think we joined St Ninians at the start of primary 3.

I have a strange memory at an early stage of school, its silly in some ways but always sticks in my mind, I'm going to share it with you, it's a wee story all about a penguin biscuit, I had a brown saddle double buckle school bag, my mum gave me a snack every day for a play piece and one day it was a penguin biscuit, we got milk every morning in school, it arrived in ten-bob shaped orange crates, the milk was in small triangle cartons with a straw, it was amazing, it was always nice and cold, so I went into my bag for my play piece and it was missing, this haunted me for ages, I was traumatised that I didn't have a play piece, I thought how did a penguin biscuit escape from my saddle bag with all the buckles like Houdini's snake-belt? I think the teacher gave me a wafer biscuit as a replacement, crisis over! I remember asking the lolly pop women and bus driver on the way home if anybody had handed in a penguin biscuit, no such luck and never to be seen again, I took a dislike to the saddle bag and dumped it.

Another occasion early into the new school for some reason I had a small, no, what I meant to say was big toilet mistake, a bit of bad timing combined with a touch of the old tex-ritters, sometimes it's not wise to ignore the volcanic rumblings coming from my belly and pain shooting to my ring, 25 minutes until the dinner time bell, will I make it? shuffling about in

If Your Feet Are Tired And Weary

my chair, being told by the teacher to sit at piece, I was ignoring the trains queuing up, then "*miss, miss, miss I need to go to the toilet*" I was already halfway out the class room door and then machine gun farting along the corridor with every step I was in trouble, then splatter, hot bisto lava, right down the short trousers and lucky for the cleaners mostly caught inside my wellies, not a very good site, I had well and truly shit myself, no half measures, full boona, I was in the toilet and no way I was returning to my class, I was pure stinking, steam rising from my wellies, I needed help, I had 10 minutes before the lunch time bell went, so I shuffled along the corridor, headed towards the medical room and said I had a sore belly and had done a wee mistake, they looked at my fake tan stains at the back of legs and smelt me coming along the corridor, waddling like a duck, I was upset and wanted to go home, they informed my teacher and sent me home after helping me clean the back of my legs and wash out my wellies I still had the shitty breeks on and sent home on the bus with a note in my hand to give to my parents.

So after getting home stinking of shite and the embarrassment on the bus, my dad was at work and mum was out shopping, so I sat at our front door waiting on my mum, then the nosey auld neighbour in the close came out her door and over to me and asked *"are you all right Andrew?* I said *"no, I've had an accident"* and handed the neighbour my wee note, I don't think it was too diplomatic with the facts:

Andy Bell

Dear Mr/Mrs bell
I had to send your son Andrew home today as he jobbied his trousers in school, please ensure Andrew has an emergency change of clothes in his bag to avoid this situation occurring again and speak to him about the importance of timing regarding the toilet.
Yours truly,
Miss Fox
Head teacher

The neighbour gave me back my note and said *"your mum shouldn't be long, don't worry, it will be ok",* then shut her hoose door, I then heard her laughing along her lobbie (hall), at that stage I wasn't caring, I was only worried about my mates finding out, thankfully the story never hit the street or playground. It's a hard one to bounce back from with street cred, if word got out you had shat yourself.

I remember a classroom mate of mine was late one morning; he never got in until 11.30am and school started at 9am, he came into the class and shut the door quietly heading to his desk, when the teacher asked him to approach her desk and wanted to know why he was so late, his reason was, classic priceless glesga innocent patter, *"well miss last night my da was at the pub and got very drunk, on his way home fae the pub, he became was very sick and lost his new wallies (false teeth) so this morning my ma asked me to help her find my da's teeth, cause they cost a fortune, and I've got good eye site and we found them, ma da gave me 2 bob",* the teacher replied *"ok sit down Robert , you did very well"* It's strange to you as a young person and hard to understand why your best mates go to a school at the top of the street (Temple primary) the one you really want to go to, instead we have to travel to attend another school, so the question of religious beliefs and faiths all meant absolute nothing to me as a young person at early stages of school or the fact that my pals could have a long lie in their beds on a Sunday morning when we had to attend 10am mass, without breakfast, so you could have holy communion and the school teachers used to look out for you at mass and ask you what the children's service was about on a Monday back at school.

Another clash was my mates joined the boys brigade (BB) because of the Saturday morning football and we were not aloud to join because you had to attend church parades and attend church. We were told to join the scouts up at the chapel hall (no chance) so boring and fuck that dib-dib mob, playing dummy camping in dossy park, no, we wanted to be with our mates in the same football team we just joined behind my dad's back and planked our BB chip poke hat and BB buckle belt, we had to keep polished the 116 and 247 to be exact, we played British bulldog, did flying angels over the horse vault and put on shows, like Joseph, we had a good laugh and really enjoyed ourselves, yes there was a bit about putting up with the attitude of some of the middle class churchy do-gooders, volunteering their time, feeling sorry for the 'great unwashed from Temple', however, within these ranks there was a great woman called Jean Finlatter who really was the first adult I ever met that believed in me and was a real gem, Jean worked in child care and adult education and was very active in her local community, she used to refer to us as *her boys*, I have no doubt we tested Jean and her young helper David Buchan on a regular basis, but she took our nonsense all in her stride, she lapped us up big time, we all respected her as did the big team from Temple, she was part of the 247 BB and Sunday school linked to the church, she didn't judge us on our background, she had something special, magic, and caring about her.

I believe I had a wee bed wetting problem when I was at early primary school, being lazy during the night I was told, I always wondered why I was not a big hit with the girls at school, and they all felt I was very funny, but never fancied me. I now clearly know why, you have to visualise, summer time I am standing there in school trying to impress the lassies, so I had shorts on, held up with a classic red and black stripe snakebelt, black wellies (July) stinking of aroma (pish) the medical room has just slapped hundreds of ethiderm on my head for the boogies (nits) I had a home-made bowl hair-cut and as I discovered later, I was wearing a shirt with big fucking horses, running all over it.

Its funny I met big Shug Glancy, fae Temple, years later, I went to primary school with Katie his sister, she was in my class, he said *"my maw has school photos of oor Katie and you are in them, I will copy it"*, so true to his word he gave me a copy, so I was studying the picture trying to remember all the faces and I clocked myself I laughed away, everybody's parents attempting to send their kids to school a wee bit tidier on annual classroom picture day, spot the odd one out, me! everybody had a shirt and school tie on because it was the top half that the photo showed, however I had no tie, but a loud shirt with horses running wild all over it, with the tap button tightly fastened I was starting to wonder why I was getting called names, such as smelly bell, boggy bell, cowboy Joe (horse shirt) or trampis from the Virginian cowboy programme.

I have no doubt it bothered me at times but I just got the head down and kept on making people laugh, in some way that deflected any focus away from me and I played good at football, scoring a lot of goals, so this gave me good cred with my peers, it was the older boys in the school who called me names, thankfully it didn't get out of hand and half of them were real paraffin lamps (tramps) themselves.

Some of my primary school classmates from memory were to include: (apologies if your missed out) Fish, (Martin Heron, great life-long mate) Sammy Hutchinson, Corky, Murphy, Shieldsy', James Harran, Kevin Manley, Paul Ward, John Mullen, Joseph McMonagle, Liam Corrie, Mark Gilmartin (brain-box) Stephen McCourt, Philip Shaw, Paul Darcy and the

Andy Bell

lassies were: Sandra Ingles, Sandra Flynn, Theresa McCallum, Theresa McDermott, Connie Cairns, Joyce Connelly, Katie Glancy, Sandra Deeny, Brenda Logan, Dorothy Tuttie, Kathleen McLafferty (brain–box) Alison Sinclair (her da was the Scottish snooker champion, Eddie Sinclair) Alison used to copy a lot of my answers, wonder why she never made much progress? I liked Connie Cairns at school, but new I was off her sights to have any chance of her becoming my girlfriend, so I didn't bother too much about the lassies, but had a good laugh with them both in the class and on the bus home. I think I was daily news for most of the lassies going home and saying to their parent *"guess what that Andrew Bell done or said today? He's terrible, so he is, but it was funny"* I was becoming the classroom clown along with a few other rogues, the bad influence mob and if you ended up in our group you were stuck in the *could do better* or *under–achievers group*. One day in primary school just after our lunch a bunch of us (10) from the same class, all guy's, all derred each other to dog it in the afternoon, not to go back after the dinner-school, I know how daft it seems, all from the same class, but that's the kind of mad things you did when you are that age, so two of the guy's bottles crashed and the rest (8) of us went for it. We decided to go across from the school in the wee swing park, it had concrete pipes, it was in the winter, frozen, rainy, windy, what a bad day to choose to plunk school, we were all huddled up in the pipes, the school bell had been and gone, should we go back in? One of the guy's would suggest, no chance, if anybody

If Your Feet Are Tired And Weary

goes back, you'll have to run the gauntlet tomorrow, suggested by a good fighter, no one argued with his suggestion, ok we agreed, so we were telling jokes and laughing away, I remember one of the guy's really shit himself, he was worried and bursting for the bog, he drapped his ring a few times, then the sound changed and we all new what he had done, he was guffing, we made him go into his own pipe. We had to stay there until the home bell went, then go for the bus as normal. We all lasted and felt good for dogging it and seeing it through, how cool are we or what? Onto the bus, speaking to the lassies in our class, I asked *"what did the teacher say about all of us missing? "Nothing, she just done the register and said nothing"*, we thought we were cool as fuck, the lassies were saying stuff like *"your all mental so ye are"* Fish said *"we know, we're gonny dae it again, it's easy and a good laugh"*.

The next day in school, first thing, the teacher took the register and guess whose name was first? *"Andrew Bell"* I put my hand up and said *"here miss"*, then she asked *"Andrew can you come out to my desk"*, off I go to spin my story, *"Andrew yesterday afternoon after lunch you failed to return to class, what happened?*, deep breath *"well miss you know my wee sister just started school and goes home at lunch time, well miss my mum had an emergency at home and couldn't make it to collect my sister, so at short notice a neighbour told me I was to take my wee sister home for my mum"* she was well impressed with my story *"that's very responsible Andrew, well done, go and sit down"* Yes! I have escaped big time, what a top story, then the teacher continuing with her register shouts *"Martin Heron"*, up with hand *"here miss", "Martin can you come out to my desk"* the fucker was crying before he reached the teachers desk, *"what happened yesterday afternoon Martin?,* he was bubbling uncontrollably, *"calm down Martin and tell the truth"*, sniffing away, he always had a snottery nose anyway, *"calm down wipe your tears away and sit down Martin"* and then, the biggest ever public grassing confession you'll ever hear in your life, *"miss, miss, I was dogging it with Andrew Bell"* the fucker grassed me, in front off the full class, *"Ok Martin! thanks for telling the truth",* I had lifted my desk lid to hide, *"Andrew Bell come out here, we are going to see the head-teacher for your lying to me about yesterday, look at the state you've got poor Martin in"* Fish got off Scott free and I got three of the belt from the heedy, I still haven't forgiven Heron for grassing on me, so that ended the big idea of dogging it for the future, especially with Martin Heron! In class we used to get listening to a wall mounted radio promoting educational programmers' for schools this often included learning songs and singing for the class I always liked learning new songs and the singing was a real good way of expressing yourself. I think my teacher picked up on this, one day we were singing, *"But I'm sad to say I'm on my way and won't be back for many a day...da da da..... I had leave my little girl in Kingston town"* The teacher was so impressed with my expression and effort at singing the song, she took me next door to another

If Your Feet Are Tired And Weary

class, spoke to the teacher and then announced, "*boys and girls I have a surprise for you......Andrew will sing a song for all the class*" what I wanted to say was.....bite my banger...but I had to smile...then I was counted in...... one, two, three...... singing in front of a full class....they were making faces at me and laughing....I felt like a pure fanny and got slagged for six months later.

I must have been misbehaving again one day and the teacher made me stand out at the front with my face to the blackboard, I was having a sneaky turn around to the front and my pals were trying to make me laugh, I was so board, I looked in the bin and saw paper rolled up, so I decided to stick the paper up my juke to make two boobs and turned around to the class, bad mistake, the whole class were rolling about, laughing, the teacher clocked me, I was caught with the boobs look, she made me stand there all afternoon with paper up my juke, facing the full class, stating "*Andrew wants to be a girl today, so he can*", the laughing had stopped, I thought to myself, I can feel another letter to my parents coming on, thankfully it never happened, I think she was content with the class embarrassment factor, anything for a quiet day I thought too myself, I will try and behave tomorrow....no chance.

I seen school as a place to have a real good laugh not as a place of learning I was learning the basics but not shining at many subjects except football, drama and singing. I was an international farter, I

Andy Bell

could drop my ring on request, farting was always funny and still is, especially when you had lots of quiet moments in school such as assembly, reading times, I could drop 3 and 4 toppers with a half a minute interval between them, the teachers head would keep looking up, *"Andrew do you need to go to the toilet", "no miss"* everybody was sniggering and then the teachers defence line, *"Andrew we know what happened before, we don't want to experience another mistake"* I would then hold any farts in like my life depended on it, my mates would say "*what's she talking about?* "*I don't know, she's talking pish, she's away with it"*

Farting did get me into bother in secondary school one day; I was in one period of library and the teacher a Mr. Shovalack a Russian guy, so the approach was everybody grab a book and start reading in silence no talking, he used to sit at a table in front of the class, we always grabbed the national geographical magazines to laugh at the big droopy tits and daft cunts with big plates in their lips, we were always trying not to laugh out loud but it was hard and sore trying to hold in your laughing, so instead of coming out your mouth in the form of a huge laugh, it escaped out your arse in the shape of a QE2 ripper of a fart, loud and proud, the full class were laughing the teacher looked up raging that the silence was broken in his class, he was trying to find the farter and rip another came out loud again, he looked in my direction, still not quite sure, the class were in an uproar , *"silence!, silence, in my class",* the teacher was shouting, then for a curtain closer, I let a triple go, he jumped up and grabbed me by the jumper and shouted, "*Mr. Bell, if you want to explode, don't do it in my class, do it in the corridor*", and dragged me through the double swinging doors into the corridor.

Going home on the bus everyday was a laugh, the usual misbehaving, arse at the window and shouting at people in the street, waiting until someone got off the bus and the bus moving away, giving them verbal out the windows, we use to open the side door and upper deck back window to set off the alarm and shouting at our mates getting off the bus, some of the bigger guy's new how to stop the emergency door alarm going off by jamming paper in the switch. So we could travel home with the back emergency window open, cock out, moon shining the whole world, we were showing off to the lassies most of the time, we all had travel passes for the bus, because we lived so many miles away from the school, one day we were giving this older women on the bus pelters and I was in there, "*Oi specky, donkey breath, has your man goat a big dobber*", and so on, she just sat there shaking her head, saying nothing, the next day in class, 9.30am, knock, knock on the classroom door in came the heedy with the specky woman from the bus, the class would stand up everytime she entered, "*good morning Miss Fox*", up with the desk lid, I knew I was in the shit, "*Andrew put your desk lid down the head teacher wants to talk to the whole class about*"……down with lid…"*that's one of them*" the women stated pointing at me , she was a temporary teacher covering in the school, "*Andrew could you wait outside"* oh fuck! I can feel another strong letter coming on, we had to get our parents to sign the letter before we returned it to school, I always tried to get my mum to sign it, even pleading with her, before my dad saw it, I also got three of the belt for disgracing the school and made to apologise to the teacher involved.

One day I ran out in front of a car, near the school at finishing time I was lucky the guy saw me, but I fainted in front of the motor and the man and women took me and my pal straight home in their car. I was upset and clearly got a big fright; they also bought me hundreds of swedgers and a beano comic on the way home for being brave. After the man went away I tried explaining the situation to my mum, she attacked me with the brush for the hassle I brought to the door and for the fact I nearly got hit by a car.

I got sent to my bed after my dinner, which was the night I had a high temperature and ended up having a terrible nightmare, I kept seeing a train coming towards me and I was tied to the track, I think I saw the scene on the *'Casey Jones'* programme, my dad was slapping my face in an attempt to bring me out of this nightmare. I was screaming the house down, I came round eventually and woke up in the morning with the chicken pox, I remember I had to sleep in isolation in an old cot, I was far too big for the cot and my legs were hanging oot the bars at the end of the cot. This provided the perfect opportunity for the rest of family to annoy me, make fun and laughing at me with all the spots and finding it very hard to speak and swallow, moondog would stick his heed in the room door and say "*ha ha you're no well and am playing with your favourite action man*" I would do my best to get my mum to give him a slap.

I got the chance to stay off school for a couple of days and get spoiled by my mum, a bottle of lemonade and a wee comic, its amazing how it starts to make you feel better, even with all the fuss, I still missed school, hated missing the football and the dinnie and all my pals I also had a bit off milking it for '*nearly*' getting knocked down out side the school.

Most days of my school experience I went over for Fish he stayed across the street from me at 21 Willow street, his mum, Betty worked in the post office and used to bring in chopped pork (choppy) and Morton's rolls inside the big post bag, all washed down by a cold bottle of irn-bru. All his brothers and sisters used to storm about the house shouting and fighting about clothes, breakfast, access to the bog, and money for school, the money for all the weans was lined up on the mantle-piece in wee neat bundles, someone would always lift the wrong Bundle of cash and all hell would let loose, Betty would remain calm, then take a pure flakey, " *I'm bloody sick of the lot of you's*" Fish's mum worked very hard, she was on her own with a big family, his dad had died when he was young.

Andy Bell

At primary school once you had completed primary five you were sent for a year up to St Ninians annex, it was 10 minutes up the road from the main school, for me it meant another 2 stops on the bus along Great Western road, the school had four classes and was a prefab tin roofed building on Moraine Ave, the school was all right and you still had your mates around you and were still able to play football each day. One major problem was the school kept getting attacked by pupils from Blairdardie primary school; unfortunately it was a Catholic and Protestant issue. The problem for us was numbers, if you could imagine our main school 10 minutes down the road was our main big fort, never did we get attacked in the main school, but the annex was like an out-post, always getting attacked with Indians, every other day someone got jumped trying to reach the school, they used to appear at playtime at the back playground fence, lobbing bricks and stones at the playground, one day we were under the usual stone throwing attack and a well known STV football commentators son was amongst the brick throwers' we lobbed the bricks back as a means to defend ourselves and I got lucky, right on the napper of the TV guys son, blood was drawn and he was carried off the battle field and I was hailed as a famous victor for that day at least, then the next day the sports commentator was up at the school wanting to know who inflicted the damage to his son, thankfully no grassing took place, it seemed to stop the attacks on the school for a short time, we managed to get reinforcements from our main school and go for a decent counter attack ourselves, I think they soon got the message and we settled the rest on the football park when we played them in the school league, school football got more interesting for us when Mr. Waddle arrived to teach us, he was a real footy fan and a decent teacher as well, it was mostly women teachers in the school apart from the jannie.

Overall primary school was great with every day different and full of new learning, drama and the odd adventure.

The Big School

After spending a year a St Ninians annex it was time to head back to the main school for the final year at primary and prepare for secondary school (the big school) I was finding it hard to imagine having lots of different teachers instead of one and learning all the new subjects and the idea that you got football as part of learning was an amazing thought, the down side was lots of homework and having to carry lots of books around for all the subjects.

It was a sad time to leave primary and mixed feelings of going to the big school; we heard all the 1st years got hit with eggs on the first couple of weeks and given a lot of general hassle, I have no doubt we all stuck out, hurling together like newborn lambs, with some of our school bags just as big as us. A disappointing part of leaving primary school was all the girls in our class we had spent the past 7 years with didn't follow the boys to St Tam's, they went to an all girls school, Notre Dame and had to wear jobbie coloured uniforms and in our secondary school the boys and girls were in separate classes. Our uniform was straight forward black or grey trousers and jumper with blazer and tie (a must) sent home without it, another challenge of going to a new big school was all the teams (gangs) from all the areas feeding into the school for example; Temple including the Bowie, Knightswood, Partick, Yoker, Langey, Scotstoun and Whiteinch, so when you put

If Your Feet Are Tired And Weary

all the scurvy, Shafton, Yoker toi ya bass, the Langey, Spacemen (Knightswood), the Culbin team, Partick and Scotstoun fleeto, it was going to be impossible to avoid trouble. I remember all the statements, "*hey your mob kicked fuck out of one of our young team*", "*one off your soap dodgers did a big dirty fucken scurvy menchie beside our train station*" and so on, this would lead to many square go's and friction between different gangs.

There was two main factors to determine how easy your passage and introduction into the big school, the first was the luck of having a few big brothers already at the school and a bonus of being gemm and a good scrapper and the second was you were part of a team in the school that had good recognised fighters and always gave hander's if any bother started, lucky for me I had a foot in two camps my pals all had big brothers and would help me out if I got any hassle, the second was I was a young Temple scurvy member and to mess with one was to mess with the full team. We had additional protection from the older scurvy team at the school and when conflicts got out of hand and had a bigger team onto us we joined up with Shafton and at times Knightswood teams, overall we had very little big bust ups between different gang areas attending the school, we all had a common enemy, other schools near us such as VD (Victoria drive) and Jordanhill (big posh school) around the corner from St Tam's, they were always up for a scrap, they specialised in the art of ambush especially if you were on your own or low numbers, there was many a time I was glad I was a fast runner, we dished out some slaps to the jobbie-hill mob, in return some of my mates got a few kicking's off the snobby fuckers, but for every ambush we responded with a hundred reply's.

I remember a guy from Temple Sammy Hutchison had wore steel toe cap boots to school, you always wanted Sammy on your side if we had a kick about at lunch time he was crazy with these boots, he held the world record for smashing through empty milk bottles all in a row against the wall (18) he just kicked with his boots right through them, big runny and bang, new record. His famous party piece was walking past the Jordanhill mob and kicking them on the back of the legs from the back with the steelies on, they would drop like a pun of shit, before starting to scream, his mum died when the family were all young, they were brought up by their dad, Sammy had a famous sister called Lizzy fae Temple, I went to primary school with Sammy I liked him at school, like us, he didn't have much but just got on with it, one of the sisters, Christine went about with Brenda, my sister, I think most of the family moved to Fife.

I remember the biggest task of attending the big school was getting back and forward to school safely, we had to pass both Knightswood and Jordanhill on route as we walked every day we mostly opted for safety in numbers when passing the rival schools. It was difficult trying to remember your way about the big school how to get from one department to another.

If Your Feet Are Tired And Weary

The other challenge for me was remembering what books to bring each day according to your timetable, including PE kit or a container for cookery, you could start to recognise your good days from the shit heavy subject days with lots of homework, an example of a stinker day, included double Math's, double English, French, History, RE, how crap a day was that and the teachers wondered why so many dogged it.

I remember PE they insisted you brought a towel into school with you for a shower after a double period of football, rugby or running, I remember early in first year I had PE it was a very wet winter morning, sometimes the class didn't know what they were doing until we got changed, if you forgot your kit you had to spend 80min writing out the international rules of volleyball. One morning we got changed and the teacher said today we are going down to Scotstoun showground to play rugby, along the natchey (a nature trail leading to the sports field the official square go venue) none of us had ever played or were interested in playing rugby, apart from the chance to kick fuck out off each other and get away with it, so the teacher arrived and we looked at the grass park it was baldy of grass, full off puddles, with mud up to our knee's, one of the lads shouted " *but sir we can't play in that"* he looked astounded *"what? don't talk rubbish, great conditions for a game of rugby"* we were all huddled together like a family of meer cats, frozen, *"right all of you's line up along the line at the side of the park for the warm-up and after 3 start to do forward roles across the mud park all the way to the other side"* I

Andy Bell

think we all looked at him as if he was off his head, totally lost it, *"right I will demonstrate"* and sure as fuck he started to forward role across the park and then shouted *"last over will do it back over again"* it worked, we all dived into the mud and went for it, then started the game and had a great laugh, everybody was minging of mud and soaked right through, some of the class were unrecognisable because of the mud on their faces, it was not a day to have forgot your towel and be second, having to share with someone after their use. It's not the first time I've saw a towel being shared by up to four of the guys and have a few burnt chicken scars after usage. I suppose throughout secondary it was always the main slagging time at PE, shower time, it was always interesting the lassies got individual shower cubicles and the boys were just flung in together. In first and second year if you had a baldy white-incher you were quite safe from slagging because most of the guy's were the same, however, if you had a dirty hairy dobber, side boxers, a big minge and hairs under your arm's you were a pure freak and given a heavy slagging all dished out by the majority of white-inchers, however, if you were a stumpy nae baws or your nut bag was larger than your tadger you got it before the hairy arse mob, it always caused fights in the changing room, some guy's got whipped bear arsed with the towels and their clothes flung into the shower, it was always taken too far, some guy's were even left in tears.

I remember one morning at playtime, sorry, it was break time it was big school, we were flinging this

If Your Feet Are Tired And Weary

guy's bag to each other, passing it about noising the guy up, he kept trying to get it back and he was getting more frustrated and grabbed me by the jumper, I said *"watch what your doing ya fanny"* he had his bag back, he said *"no will I fuck you's had my bag",* I said *"we were only joking"* he was in the same year and from Shafton, I suggested he fucks off or I would knock him out, he wouldn't back down and squared up to me, I said *"square go at 4 ya fucker"* he said *"right your on"* I was amazed, wait a minute I'm saying to myself, I'm in a fight here after school I couldn't think of backing down, my reputation was at stake I imagined he would call it off at some stage during the day, before you know it word has spread throughout the school about the square-go down the natchey at 4 it was still on big time. At lunch time I honestly expected a call off, but the word I was hearing was he was up for it and fancied his chances, at one point in the afternoon I was next class to the guy in the English department the idea of fighting after school was starting to worry me, after each period it was getting closer, I couldn't concentrate, my head was preoccupied with this square go. I was thinking what if I get a tankin? What if he batters me? How will I start the fight, what's my first move? Will I kick his baws or punch him first? Before I knew it the bell was ringing it was 4 o'clock and no call off had arrived, the fight was on and the crowds were running past me in an attempt to getting a vantage view down the natchey. I passed my the jacket to my mate to hold, the last thing I needed was it pulled over my head, the walk from the top school gate to the natchey was 3 minutes, I got there first and the crowd was growing to a 100 plus then the guy arrived with a few of his pals, my adrenalin was high, I was all going and nervous about the situation getting egged by the crowd, who started chanting "Fight! Fight! Fight!"

The guy took his jacket off and gave it to his pals, without messing about I had decided to go for it, to get it over with as quick as possible, I ran to him and planted about 4 rapid punches right onto his mush, it was that fast he thought he was surrounded, he was stunned and hit the deck I kicked him about the face and body, he had rolled up in a ball to protect himself, I was kicking and shouting "*have you had enough ya bastard*", he was screaming "*aye, aye, I give in, no more*", so to the disappointment of the crowd it was a first round tko (technical knockout) no blood drawn, I was glad it was over, I put my jacket on and made my way home, pleased it had worked out in my favour and hoping to avoid the horrible arranged square go feeling again. I did speak to the guy that week and wish him no hard feelings, the fight didn't give the school too much to talk about, so the event blew over, the guy showed bottle in the first place, excepting a square go with me knowing the potential honners I could call on, thankfully they were not required.

I had a few scraps in the big school over the 4 years I spent there but it was mainly the odd punch and a boot up the arse nothing too serious. I joined

If Your Feet Are Tired And Weary

a stage show titled 'get back' a 60s musical show I got pelters for taking part. It started as a wet lunch time joke to get out of the rain and then the promise of rehearsal time during school time was tempting enough for me, I think my mates were having second thoughts on the idea when we got tannoyed down to rehearsals during a period of double maths, I really enjoyed the show, I also liked drama and role plays, the old drama teacher lapped us up.

One of my pals, for a laugh, drapped a dirty big steamer (shit) on the main stage one lunch time, knowing we had to rehearse the show straight after lunch I kept the edgy for him; the dirty bastard even wiped his arse with the big stage curtains. I couldn't move for laughing at him, they did look into it, but thankfully no one grassed.

Whilst many of my Temple pals attending Knightswood in the same year as me, were making nice wee wooden stools and boxes for their mums, they used to work on them from the start of the year and give you an update on their progress, they even made small metal shovels, good for the coal bucket. At St Tam's we were getting woodwork but making heehaw thanks to me and Fish the whole class spent most of first year writing out of books, 4 period's per week. We had a woodwork teacher called Mr. Currrren he rolled his r's, so every time he read the register it was like a sketch fro Monty Pythons The Life of Brian, biggest dickis and who's wodger, Fish's name was Heron so it was a snigger when he called out "

Martin Heywoon", one morning Mr. Currrren opened the register and the head of technical department came in and asked the teacher to go outside for a word, so I went out to the desk and drew a big cock with a fireman Sam hat on it with a black inky right on the middle of the register (class 1B4) Fish went out and added a big set of baw's we held the register up and the whole class was in a uproar, a couple of minutes later the teacher returned to the class, we were trying to hold it together and not laugh, the teacher looked at the book, it was A3 in size, he looked at the class, there was a slight moment of silence and the teacher turned the register upside down and said to the class *"rrright boys who has been dwawing the funny face on my wegister*? He was raging, we were all sniggering away, he showed the upside down book to the class and pointed out the two eyes and the big long nose, he knew it was a dick but could not admit it in front of the class, *"ok, no-one willing to take wesponsibility? wait, I will be back"* he took the book and went and got the head of tecky, he came into the class and said *"I will give you 5 minutes to discuss it yourselves and decide if the person responsible shall own up, because if not the whole class will suffer the consequences, this means all the class for the full year will get no woodwork and write out of books"* hence the writing punishment, it was cool of the whole class to take a hit and miss out in making stuff for home, but grassing was a no, no, the teacher kept the register the same for the full year. In 2nd year we got the opportunity to combine both woodwork and metalwork, how exciting, NOT,

If Your Feet Are Tired And Weary

whilst my pals were making coffee tables and wooden lamp stands we were making, wait for it, crucifixes and crosses, fucken unbelievable a wooden cross and a lead mould of Jesus, mine came to some use, my granda melted Jesus and made lead fishing weights in spoons and I used the cross as a crossbow, it was top of the crossbow range because it was all varnished, my mates all broke their ribs when they saw our wooden crucifixes, it was a quick reminder of the religious emphasis of our school.

One day in third year I got myself into a spot of bother again, it all started at the dinner school queue, I was waiting to have my ticket checked, near to getting in and guaranteed pie chips and beans, it was a nightmare if a teacher kept the class back at lunch time it meant the back of the dinny queue and almost certain a duff dinner, cold meat and a mash tottie. One day I was so disgusted with the dinner I lifted the hot mash tottie off my plate and tossed it towards the pre-fects dinner table, it splattered onto one of the guy's neck, he was squealing like a pig and jumping around, I walked out the dinner school undetected and went to the ice cream van facing the dinny.

So back to waiting in the queue and the next thing a lot of guy's took a short cut from inside the school instead of going around the outside playground and joining the queue from the outside, they all jumped into the line next to me, so the female teacher on the dinny door started to panic and shout at the

Andy Bell

guy's she started grabbing bodies from the dinner line, "*get to the back of the queue*" and then she grabbed me by the jacket and said "*get to the back of the queue you cheat*" I said "*what are you on about I've been here waiting all the time, ask the people behind me*" "*your lying*" she said and kept pulling me out the queue, "*you are not getting in the dinner school until last, I saw you jump in the queue*" I started to loose it "*fuck off ya cow and get yur fucken hauns aff me*" I shouted to her, she was shocked, "*what's your name and class?* I was raging "*get tae fuck am telling you fuck all*" she grabbed me again by the jacket, I grogged a topper (spat) on her face, it was hinging from her nose, she was squealing, I shouted to her "*stick yur dinner up yur arse*" and marched away from the dinner room area. It was Monday the start of the week so I could flog my dinner ticket it had a full week on it, so I sold it within minutes and bought hundreds of munchies including 20 Argentinas from the ice cream van and decided to head home. I told my mum I had a sore belly and was sent home, I new I had to keep a low profile for a couple of days. The next morning I was in French and the depute heed came in the door and asked to speak to me outside, he said "*where's your dinner ticket?* I said *"I've lost it"* he said "*cut the crap Mr Bell, here is your ticket you sold it yesterday, the guy got caught with it, your names on it, we both know why you sold it*" I said "*yes I got assaulted by a teacher, that's why and falsely accused of skipping the dinny queue, that's why*" he stared right through me. "*so you verbally abused the teacher and spat on *her face, not acceptable behaviour in this school Mr Bell you could get expelled for this, however, I am only here to deal with the selling of the dinner ticket and give you 3 of the belt, hands up"*

No messing about, Bang! Bang! Bang! Real crackers, right up my arm's, he then informed me I had an appointment to see the head-teacher at 2pm the same day. I knew I was in big deep shit, the heedy was an older guy he had a big toy electric train set up in his office with wee stations and landscape, it was 1.55pm as I sat at the school reception area I was crapping myself, I was more worried about ma dad getting called into the school, what if I got expelled? What if my dads on his way just now? I would be as good as dead, the heedy's door opened, *"Mr. Bell in you come"* here we go, it was just me and him in the room he had my record in front of him including my attendance record, to give him his due he said *"tell me in your own words what happened at the dinner queue, you know this is a very serious disciplinary issue"* after I explained the story, leaving out the swearing and the spitting, he said *"you were swearing and spat on the teachers face"*, I said *"sir the spit must have came out my mouth by mistake because I was angry for getting dragged from the queue and I was swearing I was embarrassed in front off all the dinner queue"* I started to think he was listing to the issues of how the teacher was dealing with the situation, he then said *"under no circumstances is verbal abuse and spitting at teachers acceptable in this school , you have two choices, you will be*

Andy Bell

suspended for two weeks and not allowed back into school until both your parents meet with me and give reassurances about your future conduct in the school or you will receive the maximum punishment of six of the belt, you will personally apologise to the teacher involved in this incident and the matter will go no further, your choice Mr. Bell" I said I was happy with the second option, knowing I already had three from his depute in the morning for selling my dinner ticket, so it was belt from under the suit jacket at the shoulder and three in each hand, my hands were double the fucken thickness and marks all up my wrist, but I had escaped my dad being informed so it was worth it. I had to go to the teacher's class the next day and apologise and that was the end of that bad week at school, its funny how your peers think you are cool because you got nine of the belt in one day. I suppose *I* lived off the coolness of it for some tie at least until my hauns got back to their normal size.

When we started to become more settled into the big school after dinner school we used to go for a walk down to Victoria Park or go raiding for apples and plums there was some amazing trees around the school. One day we decided to give our mate a walk down to Partick, he was wanting to buy some new studs for his football boots, we just scoffed our pies from the dinny on the road down, the route we took was along the old disused railway track running from Whiteinch to Partick marine police station. As we made our way along from Whiteinch, having a good laugh, we spotted brown boxes stacked against the brick wall of a local factory, on the railway side; there were about 10 flat boxes with loose tape around them, so over we go to investigate, I ripped open the box and they were full of frozen chickens, 12 fucken boxes, we had struck gold, there was about five of us there, one of the guys said *"right guys look for old bags and help yourself, fuck the studs, we're heading home with the chickens"* so I started working out how many I needed including some to flog, I found 2 old plastic bags and filled them with around 10 chickens , the rest of the guys filled their bags and some of the local guy's were planning to return later to have another raid, then from no were these two men appeared one with a camera, he was taking pictures of us with the bags of chickens, *"were do you's think yur gone?* I said *"tell that prick to stop taking pictures of us"* the guy said *"were you going*? As quick as a heart beat and sniffing trouble a story emerged *"we are going to Whiteinch police station, we have found these chickens, there's hundreds over there"* the guy said *"no need for that guys, the police are here"* and I turned around and we were surrounded by the cops, 2 meat wagons full, it turned out the two guy's were from the factory (Marshalls frozen foods) were we had found the chickens, at first it didn't bother us, because we had done nothing wrong apart from find chickens, it worked out a few vans got tanned the night before in the factory yard (inside scam) and guess who was het for the job? Us fannies! handcuffed and into the meat wagon on route to Partick marine, fingerprints, photo's and

Andy Bell

charged with chicken theft, all of us had sound alibi's all at different clubs or at home the night before, no finger prints matching the van doors tanned in the yard the police new we were just daft boy's who stumbled on the scam, they thought about charging us with theft by find but we were clear we intended handing in the chickens to the police, basically the police were fucked they couldn't nail us for this shit, it didn't stop the young detectives clucking and walking like chickens all day past the detention room, I think we even found it funny, our biggest worry was facing our parents (my dad) who had to come from work to collect me from Partick marine, lucky for me I was out with my dad collecting his sisters Heather and Frances from their work in the queen mothers, he did it every night, so my dad new we didn't break into the vans, and it was our lunchtime when we found them, no crimes committed and we were all off the hook, we had to explain the story to the depute head the next day at school, he was beeling he could not punish us, all charges were dropped, cluck, cluck.

One of the subjects I was enjoying at the big school was home economics. (Cooking) Our teacher was an older woman called "auld Doverty" she was old school with a high pitched toffy voice, it was andrewwww with four W's onto the end, I think because she was different we all got on with her, she was strict in the class, if you didn't bring a tub in you weren't allowed too cook, sometimes we had to bring in cheese or an egg, our record waiting outside the class was six eggs in our mates pockets, have you forgot your

If Your Feet Are Tired And Weary

egg, no it's in my pocket, slap not any longer, it was cool learning to make grub and let your mum taste it, cakes, soup, macaroni and cheese, most of the time all the evidence was scoffed before I reached the house or it was sabotaged by one off my mates, bashed or flattened, it became a regular each time we walked outside the class.

On one occasion in the class we were making a double sponge with jam and cream in the middle, I always started eating my sponge mix before it got in the tray's, in the class we all had a cooking area with a working surface and all the cooking utensils, pot pans and baking trays I think we shared the cooker between 2, so in the class there was always the teachers pet, the serious arsehole, always picked by the teacher to demonstrate his, mixing technique, how clean and tidy his working area was, his dishes and most importantly his finished product i.e. puffy light sponge, perfectly cooked scones, so for us with the flat sponges, burnt scones, it was pay back time for smart arse. There was three occasions I remember getting him, the first was straight forward when he was away into the store at the back of the classroom, I turned his oven temperature up full on an apple pie, he never noticed and we could smell the burning, but we were laughing our heeds aff, then auld Doverty shouted "*boy's check those temperatures*" of course smart hole didn't budge an inch as he was sure it was some other dafty, "*watch the timing, time boys, out the oven and let it stand*" so show aff hole took his out the oven with instant escape of burnt smoke

Andy Bell

escaping from the oven, over comes the teacher *"this is not like you Mark"* his apple tart looked like a roasted rat smouldering away, we were breaking our ribs, like muttley from catch the pigeon. The second was a sabotage to his fruit scones he cooked three perfect fruit scones all light and puffy, his routine for the teacher when he was showing off was to cover up his scones with the dish towel, then attract the teacher over and grab the dishtowel by the corner and do the magic sound 'Ole' like a fucken Spanish bull fighter, what a Fannie the teacher lapped his routine up, so when daft arse was over washing his mixing bowl at the sink I sneaked over to his tray and squashed his three scones and carefully replaced the dishtowel, it was all in place for his bull fighting act with the dishtowel the teacher was soon over, 'Ole' he smirked *"mark your scones have been over cooked they have fallen apart"* astonished he stared at the *"but miss"* he stammered *"its not like you mark"* she said walking away and tutting, we loved it, he looked around knowing he was set up. The third occasion was when he was selected to cook a big massive pot of soup for pupils going hill walking one weekend, fannie hole was given the task to do the business, so under the supervision of the teacher, Mark finishes the soup and has it taken to the store room I can feel a curry powder opportunity coming on, one of the guys kept the edgy, I opened a full jar of curry powder and stirred it into the soup, as it worked out they were climbing up a Munro (a wee Scottish mountain) on a cold Saturday winter morning, after climbing to the top they helped themselves to a well earned rest and stuck into their warm soup and sandwiches, the soup was wet and warm in the flasks, *"sir it's a wee bit nippie"*, *"get it down your hatch, it will heat you up inside"*, 10 minutes down the mountain on the way back the trumpeting had started, the soup effect was starting to blow out there arses, the trains were queuing up big time, a lot of the climbing party including many teachers were running into bushes, hiding in rocks, shiting their arses off, when we heard from a guy who was there we nearly died with laughter, auld Doverty pulled up smart hole, stating the staff felt the soup was very spicy, *"that's not like you mark"*, another one for the troops, there was a rumour going about the school that I had pissed in the soup, I don't remember doing that, I got pulled up by two prefects, due to the soup story, I suggested it was a lot of *pish* and denied all knowledge.

I remember when the weather was terrible, frozen, lashing of rain, the prefects patrolled the school corridors' to prevent us from entering the school during lunch time, all we wanted was a shot at warm radiators, the fuckers used to laugh at us frozen outside, grabbing their arms and kidding on they were shaking, we were standing outside with our hands and feet frozen, some of us didn't even have jackets on, but one day it was pay back for us it was bucketing, lashing rain one lunch time and we decided to sneak in to the school via the PE department, we were all soaking wet and glad to be hurled around the radiators' in the corridor, we almost had one each, not bothering no-one, then

Andy Bell

from nowhere two jobs worth prefects, a guy and a lassie came around the corridor, "*right everyone stay were you are, don't any of you move, You know the school rules, you are all in big trouble*" they were halfway along a long corridor, I thought fuck this, I'm sick of all their shit so I grabbed the big red fire hose on the wall and pulled it out enough too blast the two prefects along the corridor. I turned the hose on and the water pressure was amazing I pointed it in their direction and the two of them lifted along the corridor they were shouting and screaming I was lifting the guy off the ground and we were all laughing, the place was flooded, they ran away like soaking rats, shouting "*we know who you are, you'll all be expelled for this*" I turned off the hose and bolted out the school with my mates. We had an October week off and never got caught or grassed for the hose job on the prefect's. I can't remember a single prefect guy who was alright they were all general bullies' with blue peter style badges, some of the lassies were ok you could have a laugh with them and some were nice looking chicks.

I was feeling secondary school was flying in year by year before I knew it was the start of 4th year, we had selected our subjects in 3rd year to start to get serious for 4th year exams. We had mock tests at the end of 3rd year to gauge the level you were pitching at in the O'level 4th year exams I was heading for C level in most subjects, however, I was in a few N/C classes (non-certificate) all that messing about, clowning around had finally caught up with me, you didn't learn much in the N/C classes but it was a laugh and the banter was great , no one seemed to take life and school too serious including the teachers, it wasn't a class inspired by personal dreams and aspirations it was full of guy's planning to play football as a career, become boxers, body-popper's or just content with a guaranteed infamous YOP (youth opportunity programme) £23.50 per week.

Another favourite lunch time pass time was going apple tree raiding we were spoilt for choice all around Jordanhill; we had the same routine every time, sneak into the garden, shake the fuck out of the tree and then chap the door looking for 'any windfalls' most of the tree was bare because we had shaken the apples to the ground, if there was no answer it was a bare arse raid at the tree, apples, pears and plums, tucking the jumper into the trousers to hold your raid I use to tighten the snake belt for extra security in case we got a chase. The only thing that messed up the lunch time apple raid was a mad barking dog not letting us in the garden. By 4th year when it came to home time we had our regular wee mix of guys and lassies all waiting for each other around the top gate, we spent most of the walk home all having a laugh, I think that meant us showing off trying to impress the girls, not in a "I fancy you or girlfriend way" I guess we were hopeless as young romantics, it was the classic always acting the clown and making people laugh a lot and people enjoy being in your company, but not really ever taking you serious as a possible boyfriend, it was more difficult because

Andy Bell

the lassies all stayed outwith Temple in Knightswood or Yoker and they were no go areas for us at night time, there was youth clubs and interest clubs like badminton and boxing in the school at night, but we could not travel too school at night, it would be like the film "the warriors" trying to get back home safe at night, we would have to pass through at least 5 gang patches.

I remember they built a new community centre in Temple near the Bowie called Netherton centre it was in lower Temple, a bit risky for us, they had security guards on the outside door when it just opened due to all the soft new seats and tables getting blagged, they were passing out anything that fitted through the swivel windows and taking off with it, including twenty big plants in tubs all blagged within 7 days of the centre opening. I went into my mates house and into his room, it was like walking into the community centre reception area, plants, soft seats, he said "*do you like my new carpet, my ma flung oot my old wax cloth*", I said "*why has it got a big white line running up the middle?* it was the carpet bowls mat from the new centre, he said "*its great in the morning no more cold feet from that fucken wax cloth*" The big white line came in handy he shared the room with his wee brother it helped mark each others side of the room.

It was near impossible to get in the new centre at night all the clubs were full to capacity, you had to wait till the weekly "your barred" list was checked

If Your Feet Are Tired And Weary

and try and get in the centre from the waiting list. As soon as we got growled at a few times by the big team from the Bowie "*whit you's wee fannies wanting doone here*" we gave it a wide berth. We had the option of a judo club in Temple primary school, the judo was pish, you had to play on your bare feet and if your feet were minging and you had holes in your socks you were in for a slagging, the only funny bit about the club was my mates went to the school and I could sneak into their class on the bottom floor and draw a big dobber and nuts on the black board and roll it up out of site, then get a real laugh when you here about the teacher the next day scrambling for the duster in front of the full class.

I remember one of the funniest blags I ever heard in Temple was when the corporation refurbished the front and back gardens in some Bowie tenement property, so a young mother staying in the bottom floor flat was for the first time getting a small garden with a nice metal fence around it with a wee gate, they laid new grass it looked the business, the women was well chuffed and let her wee boy run about the front garden, it was a million miles away from looking every day at front garden full of everybody's shit, all big holes and looking like a mud field, no chance of letting her kid in the place, so what could go wrong? a couple of days pass and the women's making her way up to Temple police station early in the morning, she marches right in the door and say's to the desk sergeant "*some dirty bastard's stole ma wean's gerrden*" the cop just looked at the women, some real scum bags had rolled up all the grass during the night and left the garden back in it's former state, no one saw or heard a thing, sad but funny, that was Temple for you, if it was not nailed down it was up for grabs, I did wonder if my mate that had the carpet bowl mat as a carpet in his bedroom had got fed up with not having the real gear for bowling and went for a real grass bedroom look.

Back at school it was getting very near the time to face the big bad adult world and leaving school as soon as you got your national insurance card you could go, especially if you were not sitting exams, I had sat four prelim exams and did ok average marks, English, history, modern studies and art. I think the prelims were in case you messed up your real exams and they had something to give you an average mark on appeal, I was pitching nothing above C, a lot of my mates started leaving we were dropping out like flies, we just got a message saying they weren't coming back to school, there was no great symbolic last day of school for me. I remember the exact moment school was over for me. I went home one day after school and my dad was talking to me about what I was intending doing, I had two months left before I left plus had to sit three exams, he said to me *"you don't have to bother with school anymore, your going to be a builder working with me"* and the very next day I had working boots on and started work with my dad, I was all excited I had to go and tell Fish I was not going to school the next day because I was starting work and he could give my highly polished

If Your Feet Are Tired And Weary

Jesus mould away I didn't need it no more, the pay deal was agreed £30 in an envelope each week, no dig money, all my wages was mine, what a deal! Bring on the world! I was no longer a kid, I was just about to receive my first steel toe cap working boots, amazing! Sammy bring on the milk bottles, going from pocket money to wages was the business!

Bogeys, Crossbows and a Dodgy bike

When it came to design, innovation and the ability to source all the right materials to make the ultimate bogey a good result turned the ordinary guy's into a local hero, it was like the great den builders they were top guy's, everybody wanted to hang about with them, I never fitted any of the great designer or builder categories, but I was a trusted lieutenant, a right hand man, a co-builder, a recognised grafter and good at sourcing the right building materials.

I think the bogey building season was mainly the summer or good weather times, light nights, so what is a bogey?, When complete it should look something like a dragster, two large wheels at the back and two smaller at the front (wheels only sourced from a Silvercross pram) or it was a poor excuse for a bogey. When you found your bogey wheels they were like gold dust, especially if it was out of bogey season, you had to dispose of the pram carcass very carefully, usually in the nolley, then find a good stash for your wheels, top secret locations, we used to see women at the shops with a baby in the pram (silvercross) *"hey misses I like your wheels they are crackers they've even got hub caps, your wee boys is getting too big fur that pram"* *"I know son but I'm hivven another wean, so the pram will come in*

If Your Feet Are Tired And Weary

handy", we would walk away, huffing and mumbling, you should learn to keep your drawers on for five minutes, end of enquiry.

So it's bogey time and you have your wheels and wood ready, we were spoilt for choice, having the widdy (woodyard) on our door step, we attached the wheels to the wood using flat bashed cans and bending the nails, leaving some movement to attach string to the front wheels for steering and used your feet against the wheel to slow down and stop, this was the basic bogey model, you could take part in the racing from the top of the street, we were lucky, Willow street had a decent wee hill, so you gathered a good pace going down the street.

It was not the first time my front or back wheels came off going down the street full flight and crashing into a garden fence and having 20 skelfs in yur arse from the wood or just missing a car coming up the street, someone was always breaking an arm in the summer from a bogey injury.

Then the great designers got to work I think their dad's helped them half of the time, but they denied it, they would appear for pre-race inspection, fully carpeted, seat attached, real break and well oiled wheels, highly polished, it even had a bogey pusher's wee seat at the back, what chance did we have racing these smart bastards, we used to take the bogey's everywhere, each bogey had at least 3 guy's into it, taking shots each at steering, pushing and breakdown repair man a real team effort, bogey's would get

Andy Bell

blagged and new wheels appearing from no where, it would cause a riot, serious fights, throughout Temple including families at war all because of the legendary bogey.

We also moved onto slings and slug-guns, it's a hobby that didn't last too long, someone always did something real bad like shot somebody's granny, fired at the police and we had to get rid of the slug guns quickly or we would get the blame. As with most of the young team I also experienced being shot with a slug gun on the arse and on the leg with a miniature dart, really fucken sore, the big team use to make us dance like chickens, river dancing like fuck trying to avoid being shot, unfortunately it came with the territory if you wanted to hang about near the big team, they were cruel bastards when they got started. We used to shoot bottles and the odd target (pigeons, dug's, cat's and windee's) We also made crossbows, two bits of wood, shaped like a cross and elastics joined together from side to side, firing wooden clothes peg's. We played at the best distance, used midden bin lids as targets and eventually had crossbow fights, if you hit anybody in the face you got a real tanking off everybody (below the neck only) even the fly shites sneaking in the hoose for a duffle coat as protection, they couldn't run fast due to the heavy coat and became easy targets, aiming for the legs and hands, I painted the top's of my peg heeds with red felty, ready for action and easier to collect after you had fired your ammo. I saw some real bad accidents and injures in my time

If Your Feet Are Tired And Weary

growing up in Temple, hundreds of broken arms and legs to lassies and boys, people getting knocked down, stitches and getting burnt.

I remember wee Tam Tolland a good tree climber, fell off the top of a conker tree and smashed his heed on concrete, the blood was running out his nose and ears, he was in trouble, a bad way, life threatening, so what does his mates do, started stealing his big conquers from up his juke when he was lying out the game, they eventually got help, poor Tam was in a coma for ages, he woke up weeks later looking for his big conkers. Everybody loved conker season, we all wanted to find the ultimate champion conker, we all had our favourite trees to raid and our methods to make the conkers solid, like steeping them in vinegar and putting them in a dark drawer for a few weeks and using smaller knitting needles to make the hole in the middle for the string, a good strong lace, then you were ready for battle, even dad's played conkers, the battle scars from the conker challenge's was clear to see, it was bruising around the hand and wrist and on the front leg from people pulling away, that costs you two shots, me and moon spent more time fighting about who stole who's conkers, I should add I was a lolly-pop stick champ, I had a 45er, this meant it survived 45 attempts to chop it in half.

Jorries (marbles) was also a great game on the stank as was chip and toss, nearest the wall with coins, then "heeds or tails" to see how much you've won, unfortunately it was the cause of a lot of fights

Andy Bell

both in school and at home. I remember we were playing with drippers, plastic bags at the end of a stick over a fire, the bag used to drip wee light bits of bag all over the place, we used to chase each other, total crazy I know, you could even use it to write a good menchie, however this guy fae Willow St, was running about with a dripper and it blew back into his face, burning plastic stuck to his face still alight, he was screaming like I have never heard, he was running about screaming for help, he ran down the street towards his house, screaming in pain, face alight shouting for his ma, he ended up with a badly scared face. I went through a stage were I bragged about not getting injured, no broken bones and then in the space of three months I had two visits to the hospital. The first was when me and moondog were throwing half bricks from the top back landing window into the blocked sour, it was overflowing with everybody's shit from up the close, jobbies floating everywhere, we were bombing the jobbies, as you do with some spare time, I went down to collect the bricks and stuck my heed out the back close and looked up at moondog the next thing, bang right in the noggin a half brick thrown from the top, smashed my front heed open, blood everywhere, I was screaming moondog arrived at the bottom of the close, pleading with me not to tell my dad it was him, I was semi conscience a neighbour came out and rapped a towel around my heed, then my dad arrived, I never grassed moondog I said it was my mate and it was an accident, 24 stitches and a fractured skull later.

If Your Feet Are Tired And Weary

The next hospital visit three months later happened when we used to jump and dive into a big giant fluffy hedge beside the ciro on Succoth road, it was part of a huge garden of which the hedge ran around the garden and linked to the wall of the ciro, we used to run along the wall and dive into the hedge, bomb each other, just like in the swimmies, the owner off the house very rarely chased us, so it was my turn to do a huge bomb into the hedge, so I go running along the wall, leap into the air into my bomb shape landing in the middle of the hedge, but unlucky for me I went right throw the hedge and landed on a steak (thick branch) it went straight through my back upper leg (near my ring) and it came through the front of my thigh, I was impelled, then the rest of my pals started bombing on top of me I was screaming, pleading for them to stop, shouting "*I'm trapped stuck and all blood, fucken get aff me ya bunch of bastards, get help, there's something sticking through my leg*" my mates eventually believed me and got help, it took the fire brigade to cut me out the hedge and then off to hospital for a small operation and six month of hell trying to get the wound healed up and no football, my leg was ok eventually, I never bragged about not getting hurt again. One of our favourite adventures was heading to the swimmies, Whiteinch baths mainly, it took us all ages to get organised and talk our mum's into giving us the money to go, we needed entry money, bus fare, although we always walked and tailed the money for swedgers, it was great if you had enough for beef soup when we got out the baths, sometimes we would collect some

Andy Bell

empty ginger bottles on route and blag sweeties out of shops, go apple and plum tree raiding, we had great laughs at the baths and even more adventures on the way back, I remember the life guards would hold your towel over the water if you stayed in past your allotted time or your band colour was up and threaten to chip your towel in. I remember cause we were paraffin lamps (tramps) and probably always shared towels, me and moondog shared a towel and it was a fight to see who used it first, I remember the guy holding up our auld washed out shabby towel over the water and I noticed it had burnt chicken or train track marks on it (skids) no doubt one of the lassies had wiped their arse with the towel and moondog just grabbed it, so with the full swimmies laughing at the towel there was no way I was admitting to ownership, I gagged moon and said nothing, I had to be 4s up on a towel that day and just told my mates I had forgot a towel. We always thought we were doing my mum a good turn by blagging carbolic soap (pink bars) from the swimmies, not realising when you used it to get washed it burned the hell out off your pork pies (eyes) they nipped for ages. Whiteinch baths still operated a steamie (a glesga wash-hoose) it had a small pool and separate big pool; it was a great feeling when you could prove to the life guard you could swim (just) and should be allowed into the big pool. I remember in the showers one day at the baths this older guy was getting washed, shampoo and soap, the works, he started washing his mortas and nuts and as wee guy's we found this very funny and were laughing, sniggering and started washing

If Your Feet Are Tired And Weary

our tadgers with the soap, copying this guy, the guy took exception to this and started shouting at us. *"you's are all scum - manky scum "* we told him to shut his gub and stop scrubbing his baws in front of wee boys, fucken baldy weirdo, we all got flung out, but it was worth it , we had our swim and it was a good laugh. There was times we never made the baths because we had spent our money, we would just go over to Whiteinch park, it had a big boating pond and wee islands, we went for a swim in the pond, it was minging dirty water, as long as we wet our hair and got the towel wet my mum would think we had attended the baths. The greatest laugh in the park was chipping in our money so that two of us could go and hire a couple of boats, row around the corner and pick up the other twelve that were hiding, six in each boat, then using the oars to soak each other and try and sink each others boats. We used to row over to the wee islands and pretend we were pirates of the high sea's and looking for old black beards treasure, sounds crazy but a truly great adventure, the rowing boat attendant (a young nervous summer £2 per hour recruit) would catch us, splashing lovers, over-crowding the boats (a form of piracy) and start to shout through a hand held loud speaker in a muffled sound *"number 15 come in, number 15 come in, you have violated the boat-hire rules, and your time is up"* and our response, because we had attracted an audience by now, down with the strides six moonshines, shouting *"fuck off ya arsehole, come and get us"* we would eventually get fed up or our boat was full of water and ready

Andy Bell

to sink, we would just jump back on land and push the boats back into the pond or sink then and do a runner.

Another part of the swimmy day away included a visit down to my auntie Molly's, she lived in Curle St in Whiteinch, she was a great women a real gem, never would she turn you away from her door, even with four, five or six pals with me, she only had a wee single end flat, she would supply the juice and biscuits for all the team, my cousins, Cathie, David, Mary, Anne and Susan all lived in the house, but were older than me. I think they just liked our patter and our daft stories. My auntie Molly was really my dad's auntie, she was my granny Bells sister (my granny Bell died before I was born) along with Auntie Suzie she lived along the street from Molly's house, but was never in when we went to the door, my dad kept telling me auntie Suzy lived in the chapel, I believed him, but I soon discovered, he meant, she was a real holy Willie, auntie Molly was really good to my mum and gave her a lot of good support, she had a wee old neighbour called Mrs. Currant, I used go for her messages, she was a very nice and kind women, my auntie Molly will always be a special person to me, she loved Elvis, John Wayne, Celtic and Italian football, a real positive person, always believed in me and encouraged me to do well at school.

Everybody loved going on adventure run's on the bikes, but there was always the same problem not everybody had a bike or could borrow one, some of

If Your Feet Are Tired And Weary

my mates big brothers would make up bikes from broken bikes lying around or if you were lucky you found one in the incinerator when we went raiding up near dossy park. Going on a bike run was another great adventure nobody wanted to miss out, even the lassies would go and that meant a good game at truth derr, some of my pals had grifters, some had choppers with a three gear change handle on the bar, one of my mates had a racing bike a flying Scotsman, once belonging to his granda and keenly restored by his dad, it was light to lift and fast as anything, but it was a racing bike and the poor guy used to get heavily slagged for using the bike because it was old, I never had a bike at the time, so I had very little to slag the guy for, it was kids being nasty, cause it was his granda's old bike, he got called the hovis kid and they used to hum the TV advert hovis tune to the guy, he eventually got a modern bike, so, for me to go on the bike run's I had to borrow a bike from someone.

I remember my pals mums saying all the time *"sorry son the tyre's flat I can't lend you the bike"* so I came across this three wheeler bike up at the dump, it was a two wheel at the back and 1 at the front of the bike, saddle and metal brake, the tyres were blown up, chain all seemed ok the only problem with the bike was that one of the back wheels were missing (back right), so to go it you had to ride it to one side like a speedway rider, it was a challenge, but apart from the slight problem with the wheel missing, it worked perfect and was very fast, I had the bike for

Andy Bell

a full summer, it must have been a sight when we had organised to go a bike run, when you looked along the row of bikes taking part, grifters, tomahawks, choppers, the hovis boy, then me "Spartacus" like from the gladiators because I had a wheel missing if you got too close to me my broken spoke would rip your leg apart or wreck your bike wheel , the only complication for me was I found it hard to turn right hand corners because I always had to lean to the left to compensate for my missing wheel, I always took a left and caught up with them, I remember the strange looks I got when I asked people to watch my bike when I went in to Martins (local newsagents) for my dad's paper, they would look at the bike and laugh, it never got stole, but what a bike! I eventually got a real new bike for my xmas one year, so it was on with the football strip at 8am in the morning and itching to get out to play on my bike, even though it was absolutely Baltic outside, weather that gave you instant blue legs and hands, steam coming from your heed, chapping my mates door at 8.30am, xmas morning *"Mrs. Heron does Martin want to go a run with me on my new bike Santa brought me, do you like it?* I am standing at the top floor of the tenement, at my mates front door, having dragged the bike up to show it off and there was no way I was leaving it parked at the bottom of the close, if it got blagged, I would have been in the oven along with the xmas turkey. Fish's mum just looked at me and laughed then she said "*it's a wee bit early son but I'll ask him" so* as promised she shouted "*Martin Heron do you want to go on a bike run with Andrew*

Bell? Fish shouted "no, *am playing striker fitty with Mick come back later*" "*ok see you later*" off I would go to another mate's door. "*Hello Mrs McFarlane is John coming oot; do you like my new bike?* "*Yes it's a smasher Andrew you need to look after it*" she said "a *will, I'm not giving any backies on it*" she smiled "*good for you son I'll just shout on John for you*"

It's bigger than a dug

I remember one day we were all up around Dossey Park playing football, moondog didn't play much footie, he was crap, so he was away exploring with his wee mates. The next thing I saw a lot of commotion at the swings area, I looked up to my amazement and saw moondog, standing holding an old donkey at the end of this long rope with a bunch of people gathered around him. I ran up to him and asked him were the fuck he got the donkey, he said he stole it from the old haulage yard near the front of the 'clenny gate'; he said that he took it because it looked very sad and the rope around its neck was too tight and hurting it, I'm keeping it, he said, I was breaking my ribs, laughing at him.

He was walking through the park with this donkey on the end of the large piece of rope as if it was a dog on a leash. He kept saying *"it's mine we'll take it hame and keep it around the back"* the crowd was growing bigger all the time, mainly children starting to clap the donkey, moondog kept saying to the donkey "Harry" (its new name) *"be a good boy"* it was similar to a scene from the bible, once the older mob arrived they started shouting at the donkey and John wouldn't let the donkey go for nothing. One of the big yins eventually slapped the donkey's rear end and it went crazy, it bolted and started ee-awing! ee-awing! but would John let it go, no chance! The donkey was off and moondog was being dragged

If Your Feet Are Tired And Weary

around the park at high speed, attached to this twelve foot piece of rope shouting, *"all you big team are cruel bastards, stop Harry your safe now"* trying to reassure it. The donkey eventually stopped dragging moondog through the grass, his cloths were covered in big grass stains, he asked me to help him down to the house with the donkey, I told him my mum and dad would kill him, and we had to go passed the police station and along the busy Bearsden Road to get hame.

So mad as it seemed off we set heading down to Temple, out the park gate and onto Bearsden road, cars were slowing down, guy's from work vans were shouting all sorts of abuse at us *"hey wee man you've got a donkey following you" "hey ya couple a fannies, Blackpool is the other way"* they were tooting their horn's and the donkey was shiting itself from all the traffic, moondog was trying to keep him calm, *"it's all right Harry you'll soon be hame"* we were getting near the police station, but on the same side of the road, we saw the blue bus coming towards us from Canniesburn and I said to moon we need to go for it when the bus passes, we have to move quick down to the traffic lights, so wee made it passed the polis station, stopped at the lights and pressed for the green man, we were getting strange looks, lucky for us no police cars in site, across at the traffic lights me, moondog and Harry, onto Fulton St, nearly hame and then moon wanted to stop at annies the fruiters to ask for a couple of carrots for the donkey, who was well behaved all the way from dossey park apart

Andy Bell

from being strange at the double pedestrian crossing, he clearly wasn't sure about crossing at traffic lights, so we tied the donkey to a street poll outside the fruiters and moondog went in and asked Annies for a few spare carrots, she asked what it was for, "*Harry, ma new friend, he's a donkey*" Annie was astounded "*no way*" she said, "*it's true Annie, ma big brothers watching him outside the shop at the chippy pole*" out the shop she came and started to laugh her heed aff, with total disbelief, and gave us four big carrots free of charge, all the people shopping were laughing away and clapping Harry, the moon gave it a bit of carrot and off we went into Willow St and stopping at our close, he said " *right let's put Harry in the front gerrdin, you watch him and I will ask my ma if I can keep him*" my dad was still at work, all the neighbours were at their windows, so moon chapped our hoose door and my mum opened the door, "*ma, I've got something to ask you*", "*what have you been uptae*" "*well ma I have found something, like a dog but a bit bigger*", "*whit shit are you talking about*", " *I've found a new family pet*", the next minute the neighbour is at the door, "*Chrissie do you know you have a donkey in your front gerrden*? "*A whit?* my mum said "*a donkey*" the neighbour said, "*John Bell ya wee bastard come here*" the moon ran for his room, my mum chasing him with the brush, "*yur fucken getting it, yur da will kill you*", meanwhile I'm stuck outside with another crowd gathering with Harry in the front gerrden and the next thing you know a police motor draws up at the close with two police in it " *right Mr. Bell stay were you are, who*

If Your Feet Are Tired And Weary

does the donkey belong to? "Ma wee brother, it's his am just watching it fur him", the next thing my mum came out with moondog, he said to the cops, "*I didn't steel it I found it wandering about dossey park, I tried to find the parky but he wasn't about, so we brought it home to ask my ma to phone the polis, we've called it Harry, and it likes the name, do you think there's a reward for finding it*", the copper looked at him "*I don't know son, but if you are telling us lies you will be charged*", the police arranged for a vet and loader to come and take Harry away, the moon gave the vet Harry's two remaining carrots and asked him to look after it, he was bubbling when the vet drove from the street, we never heard anything about Harry again, moondog asked my dad for a donkey for his next Christmas, I don't think he could find one in the shops.

Two cans, bottle of cider and the Grease Album

Now I had moved into the world of the working, with cash burning a hole in my pocket every Friday, I could buy a whole case of alpine ginger and have as many sore bellies as I wanted, even on the traditional Friday chippy night, I got promoted to a full supper to myself, I started to feel a bit grown up, giving my sisters money for going to the shop for me, treating my mum to a bottle of cream soda and a fry's cream and her favourite, a single fish. I was nearly 16 and glad I didn't have to strip lead for the weekend football and cargo money, I use to go and see Celtic and Scotland and on the Saturday night we always had an "empty" to party in (someone's parents out or working) on this occasion, it was Fish's new house down at Archerhill road in Knightswood, he had move from Willow St, by this time, Betty his mum used to work at a club on a Saturday night and never got home until 1 or 2 in the morning, the preparation for the party was simple, get your cargo organised, for me that meant two cans of lager and a bottle of cider and not forgetting the grease album. Grease the movie had been out a few months and we were all into the songs and dance routines, I believe we all got black Harrington jackets (tartan inside) and put the T birds, meaning, Temple on the back, we loved it, the grease album was the focus for our

If Your Feet Are Tired And Weary

party, it offered us opportunities for solo and group dance performances, guy's songs, lassies songs and everybody together and even the Moonie (slow dance) at the end, what a perfect party. I would work my way through my cargo, you were always sharing it with others, making up snake-bites mixing the cider and lager, I was lucky most of the time I use to get staying at Fish's hoose so I could get a wee bit bevied, but not too drunk, Fish had big sisters and brothers, they could grass him if there was much bother, but most of the time we were happy working our way through the album, everybody had their special spot or routine. When things went wrong at the party it was the usual stuff, someone throwing up in the bog and jammed behind the door, half sleeping, someone in the kitchen crying with a crowd around them getting the attention they were looking for, having just been dumped or fancying someone and they were either going with someone else or weren't interested in them. Some greedy shit had taken a few bits out of Betty's Sunday ham in the fridge, it was all teeth marks, it was getting near the time to call a halt to this Saturday's party, a lot of the boys and lassies were in cupboards, in bedrooms, in the front gerrden, out the back with their birds, Fish's big sister used to shout through the hoose *"Martin Heron, you better send your pals hame and tell them to take the greeting faced wee slappers with them my ma's gonny kill you",* then she would get blackmailed about smoking and drinking with her mates, if I stayed at Fish's, we would tidy up quick, before Betty came in and then talk about the events of the nights party.

I remember a new lassie was hanging about with us from Anniesland road, she stayed in a posh house, her father was in charge of the Kelvin Hall, she was coming along to one of Fish's famous Saturday night parties and told us she had no cash for a cargo, so we were helping her identify something of value she owned and could flog, so as wee dirt bags, we talked her into selling her horses saddle, we got a tenner on it, some drunk guy in the linden pub bought it for his daughter, he suggested he was going to steal a horse to go with it, the lassie bought a bottle of vodka and spent the rest on cans for the troops, her mum had warned her about hanging about with *"any of that bad lot from Temple"* unfortunately her daughter was up for a good time and giving her something interesting to talk about on the Monday at her posh school.

The girl arrived at the party and proceeded to drink nearly a full bottle of vodka all to herself, she was a big lassie and going for it, before we knew it she is staggering about the house, being sick in the hall on the carpet, then all over Betty's clothes horse with all the families clean school cloths on it, Fish was cracking up, she was in a bad way, we dragged her into the living room and flung her into Betty's armchair, she was crying for a while telling us all we were wonderful and she loved us all we were her true friends and then fell asleep, we kept checking she was still alive, we settled into our grease album routines and the big drunk cunt on the chair started snoring like a hippo and farting like my dad, we were breaking our ribs laughing. We tried for ages and eventually woke her up, we told the lassie who had agreed prior to the party to allow her to stay at her house to get her home in a taxi, we stood her up and she had pished straight through Betty's chair, fuck sake! we were in more trouble, the washing was already getting re-washed from the cloths horse, she got barred from the party's, we spent the next 2 hours trying to dry the chair and get rid of the smell it left behind. We didn't find it all that funny at the time, but spent a lot of time laughing about that night.

We got chased a lot of the time on route and leaving Fish's new hoose by the Yoker and Knightswood teams, they used to jump my mates travelling on their own, so most of the time we travelled in good numbers 10+, it was more difficult because Fish's hoose was right beside Culbin drive and there was a fair share of heed bangers lived there, big families up for it and when they realised a team from Temple were on their patch each weekend, they fancied a bit of action, thankfully no major clashes really happened, but the potential was always there.

The Berries (Blairgowerie)

Every other summer holiday I had the option to go up the berries with my auntie Heather and uncle Archie and all my cousins. Auntie Heather was my dad's sister, they lived in Mountblow, Dalmuir, my dad's other sister Frances married to big Danny, he was the first Thistle fan I knew, they stayed around the corner, with more cousins, Heather-Anne, Sharon, April and Daniel, however, I hung about with my cousin Michael, he was a couple of years older than me, he loved hanging about Temple and yes he fitted in well, he was a nutter, the rest of Heathers family included young Archie, Frances, Christina, young Heather and Agnes. They held the world record for freckles on their faces. The full family used to go berry picking every summer, up to Perthshire a place called Blairgowerie, Blair for short, just up the road from Forfar, made famous for their bridies, it attracted a lot of Glasgow families each year, so what was the set up?, each family used to apply to the farmers, whom owned many berry fields, the families would pick for the farmer all summer long (June-august) the farmer had constructed these camps, made of wooden basic huts with double bunk beds, sleeping up to 10 people or families in each hut, separate was the communal cooking place (the hotplate hut) it doubled up as a drying room and big family living room because of the heat from the hotplate, it had a big long brick built stove with about ten metal

If Your Feet Are Tired And Weary

hotplate places on top to cook, it was someone's job to light it in the morning and in the evening, there was always fights with adults for moving each others pots on the hotplate, including the odd pot of totties and dinner going missing, this usually caused a riot in the camp, resulting in a family getting booted out every other week.

The washing area and combined toilets were also communal with sinks and showers, male and female separate, there was always salmon hanging everywhere, freshly poached from the river running past the camp (the Ettrick) the grown up men used too use special traps, placed in the fish steps to catch the salmon, if you got rained off the berries, we used to go poaching salmon, but we used to jig, them from the deep pools, as they rested from making their journey up the river, our tackle was strong string with triple hook and weight, throw it in and jig away, we worked in teams, watching for the bailiffs, two watching, two jigging and then switching, one of the disadvantages of jigging fish it affected the per lb value of the fish to local restaurants because the salmon were damaged from being jigged. One day me and a guy from a big family from Castlemilk in Glasgow were down at the salmon leap, it was very dangerous, we were always warned to stay away from the river, the Black water was running wild and high, full off whirl pools and deep pools the rocks were always slippy, the locals and big guy's from the camp used to challenge each other to the "leap jumps" all along the river, crazy, but true, most of the other side of the river was private land.

On the day we were poaching in a lower pool, jigging away, the water current was slightly calmer, I looked along the river to what I thought was a sack or bag in the water coming towards us, as it got closer it soon became clear it wasn't a sack but a body, it was travelling at a pace I said to the guy I was with, "*it's a fucken deed body"* the body was straight up and down, diagonal, not floating flat, so all we could see once it got closer was shoulders and the back of the head, with the face bowed into the water, split second decision, do we let it drift passed or grab it? we had an opportunity with good footing to grab the body and drag it to the side of the river, I positioned myself in between rocks were the body was travelling towards and grabbed it by the shoulders' and shouted the guy to help me I was only holding the body from going any further down the river, I will always remember the feeling, holding the body, knowing it was someone and not a sack, I could see the scalp, through the hair, we were both shaking, totally shiting ourselves. We both dragged the body onto a small pebbled area, I could see at the feet one shoe was missing and what looked like the remains of the bottom of tights at the ankle area, I looked at the hand and saw the glare of a ring on the finger, it was a bad, bad feeling, the area we were at was quite isolated, nobody around and no easy route for access. The next decision was the most challenging the body was still face down and I don't know why,

If Your Feet Are Tired And Weary

we decided to turn the body around face first, 30 years later and I can still paint the picture of the women's face, there was a sudden release of air/gas from the body via the mouth, we were hanging on to each other, like a frightened shaggy and Scooby doo, shouting for help, "*Help! Help! somebody help us*" we could start to see it was a women, someone's mum, wife, daughter, lying there totally dead, her head was 2 or 3 times its usual size, with her eyes bulging out the head, there was a large gash at the side of her head, no blood, all very sad and very frightening, on the other side of the river we saw an old laird with his stick and shouted over to him to "*hey mister get help, we had found a women's body in the water*" he shouted "*stay calm lads and I will get help*" then disappeared, before we new it the police were there, the mountain/body recovery team, we were shattered, the police took us along to the camp and got the local GP to come to the camp and jag me in the arse with something to stop me having nightmares and get a sleep, I was aloud to stay off the berries the next day. Everybody wanted to know all the details, days and weeks later, but I was never keen to keep going over the experience, a couple of weeks later a local family thanked us both via the local paper for finding their mother's body, she had fell into the river two weeks before we had found her, visits to the river for me after this were never the same. One of the strict conditions of staying at the camp was having to go and pick berries each day except for the weekend depending if the farmer had

Andy Bell

catching up to do due to rain, he usually paid a bit more for Sunday picking.

The farmer had employed someone to look after the camps and make sure the families went picking or they were sent packing. I think the glesga broo men got a run down to Glasgow every two weeks to sign on and check on their houses, as most families were away for nearly eight weeks, it was always too long for me to be away from home, my dad used to come up to Blair every two weeks to see Archie and Heather, he sometimes took a fortnight holiday off work and stayed at the camp, I was always tempted to head back down the road with my dad and catch a bit of the summer holidays with all my mates. Uncle Archie was quite strict, he never let you spend your berry money on shit, I think we paid £1 a day digs for the camp and the rest was yours, we maybe on a good day picked £3 or £4 we generally saved our money and got an allowance for the weekend, he used to encourage me to save up and buy my family presents. I remember one Saturday I took a lot of savings from Uncle Archie and was supposed to buy gifts, but I blew the lot on food, sweets and hired a bike, he went off his heed and said I was getting sent home with the broo-wallies on the next run too glesga, I kept saying, *"its my money, am telling my dad on you, fur shouting at me"* he just sent me to bed and never spoke to me for a few days.

I think my first official pint was bought from a bar in the Crown Hotel, it had a wee juke box, we

If Your Feet Are Tired And Weary

thought we had made it, getting served, I was nearly 16 and fairly young looking, Michael my cousin drank wine I never liked it, he was always in some kind of a scrap in the town centre each weekend, we hung about with each other, sometimes there was trouble between the locals and the glesga berry pickers out at the week end spending and drinking their hard earned cash, a lot of the trouble was about lassies, somebody nipped a local, or a local women running away with a glesga berry picker, the Well Medal pub was a regular haunt for the dad's and mum's from the camp. The only problem about getting drunk was trying to find your way home to the camp along the low road, pitch dark and bats flying everywhere all around your heed, the walk was a good 2 miles with the river roaring on the one side of you, local taxi's wouldn't take you along because the road was so bad.

On the odd Saturday if Archie decided to open the brown leather money bag we went to the pictures and on a Sunday we walked up over to the monkey shop for sweeties now that was a real treat, especially, if we had managed to keep some money from the previous day, we had to cross the "monkey bridge" to get to the shop.

Each day the tractor driven by the farmer would arrive at the camp to collect the pickers and take us to whatever field was due to be picked, auntie Heather was always organised with the lunch time picnic, it was mainly sandwiches, orange juice, crisps

Andy Bell

and a biscuit, a common problem was it was cheese or salmon spread on the pieces and I hated both, she used to get chicken spread and ham now and again, we were always ready for our lunch, having started picking berries at 8.30am and finishing about 4pm with a 30min break at lunch time.

There was always a lot of carry-on up the berry fields, not just kids, but adult's aswell, the tradition was to rub each others faces with berries, the adults would chase each other up the "de-rails" this was the name of the walking gaps between berry bushes, the length of a derail could be up to ½ mile long. The berry fields were organised by a person called a "derailer" his job was to allocate derails and make sure it was clean picked, it was allocated to two people, picking from each side, it would depend what the berries were been picked for, if it was for the shops, we picked into punnets and tray's of 12 before you went for a weigh in, they had to be picked clean, with no bristles and not crushed, you got paid a better price because you had to be careful with the berries, if the berries were for dying purposes of which was most of the time, we picked into buckets, you could pick faster and the classic trick was pishing in the bucket to gain some more weight. Men, women and children carried out this task, once you had a few buckets, it was time to weigh-in, this was done via a tractor with low loader and scales on it the farmer shouted out the weight and his wife paid you out, we sometimes got to pick strawberries and goosegogs, strawberries, unofficially most nights.

The ultimate crime to commit on a berry field was stealing someone's berries, blagging their full bucket, the farmer used to bring in "day pickers" in buses, they were from Fife and surrounding area's, the Fifer's always got the blame for stealing berries, I saw many grown men fighting about berries going missing, people getting battered with sticks, it was a serious matter, you can always tell a berry picker anywhere, with the scratch marks from the bushes all over the back of their hands and always stinging with the berry juice pouring into the mass of scratches, some of my cousins were good fast, clean pickers with plenty of experience, everybody had a piece of string tied around their waste and a hook to hold your basket or bucket and ready to tackle the berries, we always hoped for heavy rain, so we could get sent home (rained off), lucky for us this happened often, its interesting to know that a lot of relationships marriages and divorcés developed as a result of being up at the berries, families deciding to stay on and settle in Blairgowerie. Overall I look upon my experience of the berries with fond memories.

Breed, Coal and a Sugar strike

It must have been the late 70s early 80s they called it the winter of discontent, the bread, sugar and coal were on strike, all at the same time, it created madness locally in Temple as it probably did throughout Britain, with most families main source of heating being coal and with none available the cold winter was even more bitter, if things weren't difficult enough for families we kept getting power cuts, some lasting up to 12 hours and more, the place outside was in complete darkness, games of one man hunt lasted hours, but it was very cold too hang about the streets.

So how did we all survive the experience? it took a wide range of different measures for families to get through this challenge, one of the first things to change was me getting sent to the neighbour's doors saying *"my mum said can you borrow her a couple of slices of bread for ma dad's pieces, the weans ate the bread and the shops are shut"* I hated having to do this, especially if it was my pals hoose, but with the strike, no one had much breed and my embarrassing door knocking stopped temporary, when bread, sugar or coal became available it was rationed, this always caused real fights in the streets, adults in queues, frozen and then been told it was all finished, people skipping the queues, men smashing shop front windows because they were charging too much for their bread and sugar, the local coal

If Your Feet Are Tired And Weary

men were giving lighter loads, bumping people and handing out dross coal, all it did was smoked and burned too quickly, people were stealing each others coal out the bunkers, the place was going crazy. If someone heard a shop was getting in supplies, it would cause a stampede and people getting crushed in queues, someone working in sloans was always accused of giving more to their family, it resulted in their house windows would get smashed, it was fair to say local tensions were running high.

For us we did without sugar mostly and got the odd loaf if my mum made the cut in the queues, this was once a week if lucky, we blagged anything we could get our hands on from Morton's the Temple bakers, but they were making very little bread or roll's and anything they made they guarded, so it was hard to steal from their outside cooling trays, one of my pals got caught blagging from the bakers and when we saw him he looked like Casper the ghost with all the bakers flour hands all over him, he got a right tanking.

For heat we used three methods, the first was me and my dad and moondog going up to the bluebell woods near dossey park armed with a big double handled saw and the weans Silvercross pram used for getting the logs down the road, we would cut up fallen trees into logs or cut trees down, sometimes spending 2 hours collecting logs twice or three times a week, full the pram and head down the road, this was a real adventure, feeling you were mucking in,

Andy Bell

even knowing the sawing was killing your arms, my dad used to say *"use the full length of the saw"* I have no doubt it was a pure brass neck pushing the pram down Fulton street and into Willow street full of logs, but all we could think of was the heat off the logs in the fire, that was good enough reward for us.

The second means was all the spare shoe's got burned in the fire, one of the lassies chipped a new shoe belonging to my mum into the fire by mistake, she didn't seem to bother much about it, I remember being kept off school for not having shoe's, having to wait until my dad got paid, everybody guarded their one pair of shoes from the fire. The third source of heat was me and moondog sent to all the local church jumble sales to buy fur coats for the beds and old shoe's with good thick rubber platform soles or boots for burning in the fires, we even lit the room fires it was that cold, so the coal bunker was full of old shoes, instead of getting coal you got sent for a bucket of shoes, most of them would spark and spit rubber bombs out the fire, it was funny going up to your dad all excited and saying *"what do you think about this shoe for the fire dad?* the woman at the jumble sale said, *"it belonged to a guy with a club foot, the sole is solid wood"* I'm thinking to myself, it's a cracker, so I then ask her *"how long will it last in a fire"* the woman in the jumble sales must of thought we were bent shots, walking in and asking for any club-foot shoes and fur-coats, they would just stair at us and wonder what we were about. When the power went out it we were sent to bed early, no telly, pitch dark and freezing, me and moondog were sent up to the chapel hoose to ask the priest for big candles because the lights were out for ages, it was strange sometimes when all my pals light were on and our lights were still off, now it all makes sense, we were talking cut-off and not a power cut, it sure was good to see the back of that winter and I suppose the friends of the blue bell woods (tree huggers) were glad to see the coal back, and no doubt the church jumble sale takings were well down.

Being the boss's son

When I started work, my dad was the boss, he did building conversion work for a company called Chartvey Development, the first job I was on involved the conversion of a massive old children's home in Murdock into luxury flats, the transition from school to work happened so fast, he told me to stop school one day and the next I was up with the birds, earlier in the morning, still dark, freezing, wearing an old pair of my dad's steel toe cap boots, old jeans, warm jumper, a piece box and into the van and on route to work, I managed to warn Fish late the night before, that I was finished with school as I was off to work the next day, I was "*going to be a builder*" I really had very little idea what to expect entering the big peoples world of working, in the back of this transit van with bench seats along each side, my dad used to collect all the men at different pick up points on route to the job, he hated waiting for men being late or sleeping in, he would send one of the men to peoples door if they had slept in and growl "*tell that lazy bastard, he's got one minute, or he can lie in his own pish the rest of the week*" I was kind of glad I stayed in the boss's house, not much of a chance of me sleeping in. One of the first things I had to get used to was all the slagging, the banter and plenty of it from the men aimed at me, the boss's boy; it ranged from, if I had pubic hair? Had my nuts dropped yet? What masturbation style I had? And if I

If Your Feet Are Tired And Weary

wore a fur-lined balaclava whilst I was doing it? And their favourite enquiry, if I was back scuttling with a girlfriend and what else I was getting off her? (I had no bird, but I was telling them nothing) The favourite hobby was drapping their rings (farting) in the back of the van first thing in the morning, bragging about how bad their guts were and how last nights late night ruby murray (Currie) helped them deliver a good fart, they would even be into self-congratulating their own arse, *"good arse "* they would say, *"thought you were deed, deep breath's guy's, gets rid of the smell quicker"* the rest of the van were all boaking, with their eyes watering, banging on the side of the van, pleading with my dad to pull over, he would laugh away with the farter, breaking their ribs.

I thought they were all animals when I just started, they all stunk of booze from the night before and bragged about how much drink they had, how drunk they got and what they got up to with women, they were all real characters, who slagged each others profession (trades) and of course they all had nick names. They were all professional exaggerators, one guy who stuck out was *bear back Chic* the tiler, his work was dodgy and slow as anything, but he was more famous for his stories.

He used to drink most nights, he would drink a glass of whiskey (a double) at a time so when it came to dinner time the stories would start, the rest of the squad new how to start Chic off, they would casually ask , *"go for a dram last night chic after work?* "*yes of*

Andy Bell

course" Chic replied, *"sink a few did ya?*, Chic would start the story *"14 glass, (28 half's) walked home, had my tea, finished wallpapering the bathroom, took the dog out a good walk, nipped in for 6 quick glass (another 12 half's), went home, watched a film and went to bed, a real quiet night"* the men were all sniggering, *"what about that old neighbour of yours who wants a piece of your arse, have you been over with your Baw-flashing, bird magnet, tight Saturday night fever breeks and crutch less red Indian war dancing pants on, get over there chic and show her your two big bags of grout",* clearing his throat he replied *"no am still working on her but I have a plan"* the guy's were are all laughing there heed off, Chic was 16+ stone with a big pot belly, the squad were having to leave the room, so they could really laugh aloud outside.

So why bare back chic? Well, the job up at Mugdock was surrounded by lovely countryside and fields and right beside the job on the grounds was a big grey horse in the field, but the discussion took place back in the *howff* the place were we all met at lunch time, Chic was on a roll telling a story about his last family holiday in Spain, were he was boasting about his side-saddle horse riding, up and down a very steep mountain, he said everybody else on the trip was falling off or very frightened, but Chic was in full control, choosing to ride bare back and side—saddle, he said bareback riding was his preference, he had read in a cowboy book it help's with the relationship between the rider and the horse, so the guy let him

If Your Feet Are Tired And Weary

ride without the saddle, the guy's as usual were sniggering away, keeping Chic going with the story, the guide was so impressed with his riding, he let him lead the party and offered him a position, stating he could use a real old fashioned ranch-hand like Chic, in fact the guy re-named him "chiceeto" because he could ride a horse like a famous apache Indian, Chic declined the job offer because he was half-way through decorating his hoose, but promised to keep in touch with his new Spanish horse trail friend. The men were choking on their pieces, that's are when old Colley the landscape gardener fae Maryhill suggested to Chic that he gives the guy's a wee demonstration of his riding skills.

To our total surprise he agreed, so we all went out side to the field were the big grey horse was, Chic was trying to climb over the gate to get into the field, but found it hard to get his belly over the top of the gate, all the whole job was down watching and laughing away, old Colley had managed to get the horse over and was holding it with its mane, the horse didn't look to happy, so Chic started to try and get on the horse but he had no chance from the ground, so one of the guy's came over and tried to gave Chic a puddie-up onto the horse, he still struggled with his big belly, the guy's were shouting *"c'mon Chic, take control, show us your bare back skills"* so what they settled on was Chic lying across the horse, with his heed hanging off one end and feet dangling off the opposite, then old Colley let the horse go and slapped it on the arse shouting *"go on boy"* the horse bolted with Chic on the back, screaming, trying to hang on for life, then the horse, bucked chiceeto into the skyline, 15 feet up into the air and bang! Chic had landed, "*help!, help!, ma back, ma neck*", the whole squad were dying with laughter, unfortunately, Chic was hurt and the next thing he was being lifted in the ambulance, neck brace, back board, luckily it was only his pride and bear-back riding reputation that was seriously damaged, my dad had a laugh trying to tell Chic's wife on the phone he had a riding accident at work and was on route to hospital to get checked out, it was back to work for the rest of us, so now you know who and why we had a bare-back Chic in our working ranks.

I always found it hard to shout through the building site "*da it's the phone for you*" so my way was to shout "*John*" in a coal mans deep voice, so I didn't get slagged, my experience was to spend three months at a time with all the trades, joiners, sparks, plasterers, I was starting to chip in to the slagging and fart as good as the rest, I suppose I was starting to settle into working life, they stopped sending me for a long stand, a left handed screwdriver, or collect the tartan paint from the painter, the slagging never stopped, by this time I was now, according to my farting workmates, gay and officially scared of the beard, they kept saying they were going to set me up with an old whore for my xmas, so I boycotted the xmas night out, I started to spend dinner time messing about in the dumper, driving about the building site, they used to play

If Your Feet Are Tired And Weary

tricks with each others pieces and went through a phase of breaking each others flasks. There was a wee plasterer from Bearsden who stayed with his ma, he was in his late 20's and got slagged rotten for it, his ma used to make up a perfect piece box all neat and tidy, everything was in place, one day the guys put a dildo inside his piece box, we were in the howff at lunch time when the plasterer came in and opened his box at the big table as usual, he looked and stared at the contents, he had a piece of chicken breast on the bone, everybody was watching him, he picked out the dildo and started shaking it as if it was a salt dispenser all over the chicken, he was looking at it again, the men were bursting their guts laughing, the plasterer soon realised what was going on and felt just a wee bit silly, but took the joke well.

We had a plumber who used to go for a sleep, most days, under the floor boards and appear for his lunch with the hair all sticking up, clearly just woke up, he always got pelters from my dad, but he always denied it, he must have been good at his job to keep it.

When a big job was coming to an end it was always sad to start to see the men getting laid off as we were awaiting another job starting, all the good laughs, stories and characters all starting to disappear week by week, most jobs ran over the planned time, I was starting to really like my job and learning new skills from all the different trades including adding plenty of new patter and stories to tell my mates at the weekend parties.

Michael No butter Cairney

My cousin Michael worked with my dad, he used to stay with us during the week in Temple and go home to Mountblow at the weekend; he was a wee bit gallus, liked the wine, a bit cheeky and had a quick temper, a combination that always landed him in some sort of trouble.

I remember on one occasion I was sent to the chip-chic-in (chippy) on Fulton street late at night for my dad, he needed tobacco, so Michael said he would go with me, he fancied a roll 'n' chips, we got to the chippy and I got served first , Michael asked for a dry roll 'n' chips, he hated butter the women serving him gave him his roll, he said *"that roll has butter on it, I don't want it, I asked for a dry roll"* the woman said *"I never heard you, you need to take this one, I'm not changing it"* I could see he was loosing the rag, *"get it changed"* he said *"no, your obviously not listening to me I'm not changing it"* she said, he was raging and said *"get it fucking changed ya boot"* again she replied *"no"* Michael trying very hard to keep it together said *"just geez ma money back"* she stared at him right in the face and said *"no we don't give refunds"* he grabbed the roll and chips off the counter and hit the women in the face with it and shouted *"then you fucken eat it ya cow"* it hit the women right square in the face, she was screaming with the roasting hot chips stuck to her heed, little did we know two police were in the back shop talking to the owner and listing to the dispute, within seconds, they were out the back door and on top of Michael, he was going off his heed, they hand-cuffed him and told me to get on my way, he was on-route being dragged and shouting for his money back to Temple police station, I had to explain to my dad that he had got the jail and told him what happened, my dad went to the police station and eventually got him released in time for work the next day. It's strange but Archie and some of the family don't like butter either.

I remember one Sunday me and Michael went to Sunday school at Anniesland cross, we called it the CYC, if we attended we got a free pass for Church street baths on a Tuesday night, none of my mates were there, the next thing we knew in came most members of 'Roaches gang' from around Sutcliffe St and clocked us, we were told we were getting dun-in (battered big time) there was ten of them and two of us, I said to Michael "*we will have to do a runner out the door, when we get the chance*" the CYC was right on Anniesland Cross it used to have a big sign saying "*Christ died for our sins*" outside above the entrance. We had to clear a double busy road as soon as we got out the door, so off we went, out the door with they bastards chasing us, both of us cleared the first road and Mick got smacked with a car on the second road, he got dragged with the car for a couple of hundred yards, before the driver realised he was under the car, I kept running, all the way up to Temple, I couldn't go home, I new I would get the blame, I didn't know whether Michael was deed or alive. I went to uncle Andy and told him, what had happened, he called my dad, they both headed down to Anniesland, I was shitting myself, the injuries to Michael were a broken leg, broken arm and stitches in his heed, he was lucky, we got Roaches team back big time, Roachie himself got a tanking for it. When Michael got out of hospital me and my dad went up to his house to see him, he had crutches to get around; he invited me up stairs, whilst the adults were, chatting and having tea, we were in his room, he shut the door and said to me "*right it was your fault I got knocked down so, I want you to take 5 punches in the face, from me, with the boxing gloves*" and produced these boxing gloves, "*then it will be forgotten about*" he said, I suggested it wasn't my fault, but we could fight with one glove each, he agreed and I just smacked him right away into the air and down he went, screaming about his arm and leg, the adults appeared I still had the glove on and Michael was on the ground screaming louder, I got a battering from my dad and blamed for causing more hassle for Michael, no chance of trying to explain the story, they just reacted to what they saw, me with a boxing glove on and Michael on the ground with a broken leg, broken arm and so called, upset, we soon got over the fallout, he recovered well, we tended to always get on and had some great laughs together, hanging about with each other for many years after that.

My dad, Andy, Heather and Frances all have the same sense of humour, they loved the under dog, the guy who always got caught, they always laughed at other peoples misfortunes, like woman with moustaches and even men that got black eyes off their wives.

Hail Hail in the jail

One weekend my mum asked me and the moondog to go up the "barras" (a large famous market in Glasgow), it was a Saturday morning, I had a rough idea how to get there, but moondog didn't have a clue, so we set of with £20 from my mum, our task was simple to buy 2 pairs of shoes for ourselves for school and the winter.

When we arrived at the barras we decided to go to a wee café as a treat and buy a big roll and sausage and a juice each, we then set about finding and buying 2 pairs of shoes, we eventually settled on 2 pairs of kid-on mountain boots with fur around the edge and hook type lace design, we managed to get the guy down to £12 if we bought 2 pairs the deal was sealed, this was the way of the barras you could "haggle" (negotiate) your price, before we knew it was nearly 1pm and the Celtic football fans started appearing all around the barras area, they were heading to Parkhead the home of Glasgow Celtic Football Club, along London road, it was getting busy with lots of fans, so I suggested to moondog we follow the crowd and go to the Celtic home game, we still had £6 change, so off we went and started following the crowds of supporters, joining in with song's all the way along London road, no hats or scarves, didn't even know who Celtic were playing, until I bought a match programme, just to prove to my pals we went to the game ourselves, it turned

If Your Feet Are Tired And Weary

out to be a home match against Kilmarnock. As we approached the stadium I said to moondog we had to plank the fur boots we wouldn't get into to the game with them, so we hid the boots in the bag in a bush near the stadium and remembered the bus stop land mark, we planned to go back and collect them after the game, it was building up nicely, we followed the crowd and ended up at the "Rangers end" the away end. I think that I paid in and moondog got a lift over, this meant a man lifted him over the turnstile and in for nothing we headed into the terracing standing only (no-seats) we felt great looking onto the park, listing to the fans singing away in the "jungle" (a big shed for the Celtic home fans) the scarf's were held up for the famous song *walk on* the players were out and the game ready to start, I couldn't believe just 2 hours earlier we were searching for bargain shoes in the barras and now we were standing in Celtic park soaking up the atmosphere, moondog was also loving it, he was on my shoulders for the start of the game, we decided to stay near the front of the terrace, it was less crowded, the away killie fans were up at the back, not many, maybe 30 or 40 at most all surrounded by Celtic fans, they were all dressed like punk-rockers, they were all pogo-ing, jumping up and down like a family of merecats, singing away, we were still a fair distance from the away fan's, the banter was flowing between fans, then Celtic scored 2 quick goals and you could sense the atmosphere slightly changing, it was 20 min until half time, then another goal, ya beauty, Celtic 3-0 not even half time yet, then to rub salt into the wounds 2 more goals before the half time whistle 5-0 to the bhoys, basically game over at half-time. The Kilmarnock fans started grogging (spitting) at the Celtic fans, they were still bouncing away, then a fight started between the fans, this was happening all at half-time the rest of the fans were booing and singing *"hoollie, hoollie, hooligans"* in the direction of the trouble, the fans including us were facing up towards the fighting the next thing the police were on the scene they arrived from track side and made their way into the terracing towards the trouble spot at the back, then from no where a young rookie cop grabbed me by the arm and said *"right your jailed"* I was stunned, *"whit fur, I've no done anything wrong"* he said *"move you threw something I saw you"* my brother was panicking, it was all happening very fast, he had no money, didn't know his way home, he was on his own. I pleaded with the polis to let me go, by this time moon was crying, hanging on to me, saying to the police *"let my big brother go, let him go"*, I was getting dragged onto the track side and under arrest, I managed to give moon a £1 to get home, I asked the police if I could take my brother with us as he didn't know his way home, he ignored me and another cop grabbed a hold of my other arm, I was shouting to the moon who was left alone in the terrace, *"leave the shoes John, go straight home"* he was 15 and I had just turned 16 the next thing I was in a cell under the main stand, for the record if I had done anything wrong I would admit it, but the truth is the young cop shat himself and didn't fancy having to go into the trouble area, so he grabbed a body to get out as quick as possible and I was that

If Your Feet Are Tired And Weary

body. I was worried sick about moondog I imagined the police would just let me go, when they realised it was all a big mistake, no chance, I wasn't scared but feeling sick I wanted to speak to a higher police and explain I had done nothing wrong and tell him about my brother left alone in the terracing, but I was refused and told to shut up, what made me angry was the young cop told the sergeant I caught this idiot throwing what looked like a bottle towards the away fans and arrested him. I pleaded my innocence but no one was listening, I was wandering when I would be let go, I thought, hopefully before the end of the game, so I can try and find my brother, but to my shock the police said to me I would be held in custody until Monday and moved from Parkhead to a local police office in Tobago street in Bridgeton. The game had ended and more fans both Celtic and Kilmarnock were in the cells, I could not believe what was happening to me, the next thing we were all handcuffed and put into a big police van, I was starting to really shit myself, what would my dad say? One of the guys told me we would have to do a weekend lie in and appear in court on Monday, it was only Saturday afternoon, how would I survive being locked in a cell all weekend? When we arrived at the police station in Tobago street it was an old fashioned building, we were taken in a back door and individually charged at the desk, I told the sergeant I did nothing wrong, he just said "*everybody tell's me that story son*", I was charged with a breach of the peace, photographed and fingerprinted (processed) they called it, empted my pocket (£1.70) in cash and

Andy Bell

a receipt for our shoes, this was my only possessions, they were put in a bag and I was led away to a dark, cold cell, given a grey itchy blanket to lie on a concrete type bed, built into the floor, if that young cop who arrested me, ever reads this story, I hope he is fucken proud of his shitbag actions of that day, it was the day his police career ended not started.

I was sitting in the cell wondering if someone would come and rescue me from this nightmare, time dragged by the hour, we got offered the option of a pie or fish supper for our dinner, I picked a pie supper, but was too sick with worry to eat it, I would react to every door opening, hoping this was the time I was getting out, I was sure my dad would find me and get me out of this shit house I was being held prisoner in. Then about 9.30pm on the Saturday evening my cell got opened and the turn-key (police) informed that my dad had been to the police station demanding to get me out, but was refused as I was been held until a Glasgow sheriff court appearance on the Monday morning, he said my dad would hand in a set of clean clothes on Sunday for my court appearance and just before closing the door, he added and *"by the way yur brother made it hame alright"* I was so glad to hear that news, I thought he had anyway with my dad appearing at the station but it was good re-assuring news under the circumstances.

Then from 10pm on the Saturday night all hell let loose, the drunks from the streets and the pubs were starting to arrive, mostly blootered steaming and

If Your Feet Are Tired And Weary

shouting all night, I was surrounded by them, I didn't sleep much that night it was as miserable as you can imagine I was really shitting myself, before I new it was 7am in the Sunday morning I was gubbed and Sunday turned out to be the longest day of my life, I had been stuck in the cell since Saturday afternoon. Then on Monday morning at 6.30am I was given clean cloths my dad had left for me, it would have made me laugh, if the shirt my dad left for me to face the judge had horses all over it, but it hadn't, the police then put all of us into holding cells ready for the transfer to the big court bus that was due at 8am, before we knew it, all hang cuffed, then a short journey after collecting other prisoners from a few other police stations on route to the court, driven through big black security gates and put into cells at Glasgow sheriff court, then it was a case of seeing a in-house lawyer, going over your case and deciding your plea, I was clearly pleading not-guilty, you then had to wait until your case was called by this time you have a copy of your charge, the lawyer told me I would get released as I had no previous convictions or outstanding warrants, I was in a holding cell about the size of a lift with 6 different people all in for different offences, they were all gasping for a fag, I didn't smoke so it didn't bother me, then this lawyer walked passed our cell looking for a prisoner needing to confirm an address for his release, he was smoking the remains of a snub cigar and a prisoner from our cell said *"hey big man, don't snub oot that cigar, gee's it in here we're gasping for a fag"* to my amassment he gave it to the guy in our cell, through a small window hatch and they set about putting out the cigar, another guy had skins (cigarette papers) and broke up this snub cigar and made 5 roll-ups the place was stinking of cigar smell, the roll-up's were Barlinnie specials (very thin) but the guy's were smoking them as if it was their last requests.

About 2pm my name was called and I was led up stairs internally and appeared from the floor area of the court room in front of a judge and within 5 minutes confirming my name and address and pleading not guilty I was released with bail conditions not to get into any bother between getting released and a court trial appearance, I saw my dad in the court room at the public galley, I was glad to get out of there, what an experience, straight home and a bit of home comforts, I went to get the new shoes we planked and they were missing, I had the receipt so my mum believed I had bought them, when I explained the whole story my mum and dad laughed it off. Moondog was more excited to know all about what it was like; did I meet real bad people? Was I scared? Did I get a battering off anybody? Did I get any food? Was I chained to the cell wall? The worst thing about this whole experience was the nightmare didn't end there, when I got released after the court appearance, I moved within a couple of months from Temple to a new address, but the court sent out the citation with a date to appear for a trial to my old Willow Street address, so it was a non- appearance at court and issued a warrant for my arrest again.

So a few months on I was down visiting my mates in Temple, it was a Saturday and we were hanging about the off sales trying to get some one to get us our cans and cider for a special Fish grease album party and the police turned up and started speaking to us about what we were up to, they then asked me my name and address I gave my new address, he said "*I will check this out on the radio*" and it came back in minutes I had a warrant outstanding for my arrest, the next thing I was hand cuffed to a shop window grill and taken away to Maryhill police station, again this was a Saturday and had to do another long-weekend and appeared again on the Monday. After my lawyer explained the circumstances about moving house, I was released on bail condition again, after having spent about 6 fucken shitty days in total because of a shit bag cop at Celtic park.

To really finish this sad affair off the prosecutor fiscal sent me a letter three weeks later admonishing me and saying he was taking no further action, the case was dropped, yes I was glad, I had no criminal conviction, but raging for a long time over my hail hail in the jail experience.

He's leaving us

It was 1979 I had left school, started work and feeling a wee bit grown up, starting to buy my own clothes, had money in my own pocket, spent less time hanging about the streets at night, mainly due to being knackered from work and getting up a lot earlier, plus a lot of my pals had already left Temple, but still returned at the weekends to hang out, they were all re-housed because of the demolition of upper Temple, it was getting much to closer to us, our street was starting to empty, close by close, and offers to re-house our neighbours were arriving by the day, the first offers were always shit, in dodgey areas, like the Drum and bad parts of Shafton.

Work was going well for my dad; he was making good money with plenty of work lined up, I remember it was during the Glasgow fair me and my dad were off for two weeks holidays. I went with Tam Murray to Scarborough for a week, his sister Linda took Shirley her pal, they were a wee bit older than us, it was a great holiday, plenty of laughs, infact one night, we were out and returned to the caravan and started laughing for ages, Tams mum and dad thought we were up to no good, I don't think we had any fly drinks, It was just one of those unexplained funny moments, but the laughing when we returned to the caravan went on for a long time the lassies were even rolling about, Jean and Mick eventually decided to join in, after eliminating all the possible things we

If Your Feet Are Tired And Weary

could have been up to. When I returned from holiday I headed up to Blairgowrie, berry picking time again, to meet up with my cousin Michael and his family, my dad was already there, we spent a week there and it was time to head home and back to work.

After a few months back at work, one lunch time I was messing about with a hired ford van belonging to my dad, I used to drive it up and down the street, my cousin Michael was in the van giving me driving hints as he was well advanced with his own driving lessons, I went into the glove compartment looking for a tape and came across a plastic bag full of jonnies (durex) I was shocked and surprised and turned to Mick and said "*whit the fuck are these fur, why has my da got these in his van?* Michael looked at me and said "*I don't know how to tell you this yur da's got a bird, he met her up the berries in the summer, but the relationship has continued and she's now up the cookie (pregnant)* I gulped with shock and said "*your fucken joking Mick*" he said "*no, I'm sorry, but it's all true, she's my fucken cousin*"

I was numb, stunned, in disbelief, break time was over it was time to start back work. My head was all over the place with this information. Michael pleaded with me not to say anything or tell my dad he had told me the story, I agreed and stayed out my dad's way all afternoon, I was angry and very sad about the news and started to feel very sorry for my mum. It was soon home time, I was in the van with my dad going home knowing the information, I kept getting drawn towards the glove compartment, knowing what was in the bag and thinking to myself, he obviously didn't bother using them, I couldn't look at my dad, I so wanted to say something to him, but couldn't find the courage, we were home before I knew it. My insides were all going, my stomach was churning, I had already decided to tell my mum, it's one of the hardest things I have ever done, but I was gutted and felt she had a right to know. We went into the house, my mum always had the dinner ready, I went into the kitchen, shut the door and told my mum that my dad had a bird, a young lassie, he met up the berries and has kept seeing her every weekend and now she's pregnant, I never told her how I knew, I finally pleaded with her not to tell my dad. I was crying delivering the news to my mum, she was sobbing then she got his dinner from the oven, said to me "*get out the bloody way*" pulled open the kitchen door, stormed into the living room, my dad was in his chair awaiting his dinner, reading his paper, boots were off, I was in the kitchen with a towel over my head pressed against my ears, shitting myself, then smash! the plate of dinner against the living room wall in my dad's direction, "*ya fucken dirty whore maister, your seeing that young lassie ya bastard and she's fucken pregnant*", "*what are you on about*", my dad said, "*who said that ?*, my mum said "*Andrew just told me in the kitchen*" by this time I was listening to the rammy from the living room, when I herd my mum grassing me, I couldn't believe it, my da said " *he's trying to split us up, he's telling lies, don't believe it*" he had panicked and

If Your Feet Are Tired And Weary

said what ever came into his head, by this time I was in my room hiding, I don't remember a lot of family being in the house, my dad grabbed his jacket and left the house, saying *"I'm away out"* I heard him shut the door, my mum was crying, sobbing, in the living room, all alone, I put my arm around her and said *"it'll be ok ma, don't cry, don't worry, I'm sorry for telling you this bad news"*, she said, *"its nothing to do with you, I knew something was going on, he's a bastard"* she eventually stopped crying and asked me to go and shout on the lassies, they were all out playing and time for them to come in, I never said anything to the lassies, but told moondog, he sat in our bedroom, watery eyed, in silence and just said nothing.

A few hours later my dad returned I went to my room, my dad decided to confess to my mum about the affair and confirmed it was true, his bird was pregnant, he was crying, sobbing and kept saying, *"I'm sorry"* then he delivered the final blow to my mum, *"I'm leaving you, as soon as we get a new hoose, I will help you move in then I'm leaving"* my mum was broken hearted, I was listening but couldn't really hear what was being said. I heard my mum in the kitchen, everybody was creeping about the house, I went to the kitchen to see my mum, she looked at me with tears streaming down her face and sobbing said *"Andrew, I have something I really need to tell you, yur dad's admitted everything, he is seeing that young lassie and she is pregnant, as soon as we get another house he's leaving us"* I said *"no way, no way

Andy Bell

not my da" I bolted out the front door, feeling myself filling up and started to run down the street, crying my heart out, uncontrollable tears falling down my face, I kept running in whatever direction, crying out aloud, catching my every breath, I couldn't believe my dad, my hero, the greatest guy in the world, the person I was so close to and respected had decided to leave us, not just my mum, all of us. I kept on running and could not stop crying, at one stage I was shouting out loud *"ma da's leaving us"* I ran a couple of miles, it was like a scene from the film Forrest Gump, then I just stopped and the tears stopped, I had no more left, I met Fish on the way back up the street, I still had the greeting hiccups and said *"fish see my da, he's leaving us"*, he said, *"is he, how long fur?* I said *"forever, he's got a burd and she's up the cookie"* I went into the house and straight to my bed. I was wondering how I could still work with my dad, I had no intention of looking or speaking to him because of what he had done and his decision to leave us, and that was how each working day was, total silence between the two of us, I stayed out his road, made a choice to avoid him. Michael was worried that my old man would find out it was him who told me and couldn't get over the fact that I went home and told my mum what was going on.

It was a similar atmosphere at home, each night we went into the house and it was like walking into a funeral parlour it was like a bereavement in the house, no one speaking or having fun. Our family had died, it wasn't a death in the family it was the death of our family as we new it.

Within two weeks we were offered a house in the Drum (Drumchapel) 11 Jedworth Ave to be exact, I automatically assumed he would refuse to accept the house, it would be like suicide for me coming from Temple and moving to the Drum, I knew nothing about it, had never stepped one foot in the place, but my dad had another plan, he was off to start a new life, so to my total disbelief he decided to take the 1st shit offer.

I was devastated, it was a 5 apartment all in one level, it was ok for him he was off else where, you think things can't get any worse, he agreed a quick entry date 4 weeks, I pleaded with my mum to tell him to knock it back, we would get a better offer, but he was on a mission and listening to no one. There was two final decisions related to my dad's departure from our family and arguably the harshest my dad made the first was related to the disturbance payments families received because they were forced to move due to the demolition, it was for floor covering, re-decoration, removal costs, it was around £700 reasonable money in 1979, but my dad took it, hard to believe, but, he had a new house with his bird and decided it was his disturbance payment, he had paid the rent, so it was his, I thought to myself, *when is this nightmare going to end* then the final insult to all of us, but especially my mum, my dad then

Andy Bell

gave her a £1 of which equates to the value of 15 pence for each of us, towards bus fare to the social security office at Anniesland to inform them that "her man had left her", we had very little furniture, a new house, no money, my mum had never been to the social in her life, hadn't a clue, the new hoose was bare with a couple of beds and a big box of woodchip wallpaper left for me to start wallpapering. We were stuck in the Drum, new nobody, considering all that had happened I had to still work with my dad, but this didn't last too long after his departure. I remember my mum asked my dad to take moondog with him as he was going through a bit of a crazy stage in his life and was a bit too much for my mum to handle at that time, he refused. It was equally difficult for the lassies they were all really young, still at school and confused with the whole experience, their daddy had left them to live with another woman. I have no doubt my dad was hurting and sad about the decisions he choose to make, including at times some, I believe selfish decisions but in his own heart and mind he had already decided to move on and start a new life with a new family.

When leaving Temple I took the sign off the street "willow street" my close no 32 off the wall prior to leaving, I didn't have much time to think or grieve about leaving, it was all happening far too quick, all my mates were shocked by our move, especially worried because it was to the Drum, I had tears running down my face, leaving my home officially for the last time. This was a very sad time in my life and for all my family; it would test us all and challenge the strength of my mum to see it through.

Its not been easy reflecting about sad times and describing situations that don't make people look or sound all that nice, that's why I found it hard to cushion the reality, the effects my parents marriage break up had on all my family especially my younger sisters and brother, a lot of hurt and anger they would carry, understandably, but sadly for some, into their adult lives, but mostly the impact and deep personal let down, it would have on my mum, still present in her thoughts and feelings 30 years on.

The long-lasting personal memories, emotions that would affect any family having been through this type of difficult real life experience unfortunately it would also come at a price, an impact and lasting damage towards all our future relationships with my dad, our family were no different from any other, we all had lost something different when my dad left, some more than others, for me it was simple, it was the time in my life when someone stole my dad from us and I couldn't even report it to the police. So officially I'm just a big boy who still and always will love his dad, with the only difference being his gold star badge has fallen off.

I had spent most of my young life growing up, looking and following my dad, my hero and with him now gone and no longer in my sights, I discovered someone equally very special, my mum, I had

Andy Bell

overlooked her, loved her, but took her for granted for many years, she existed, only in my dad's shadow, but now she was standing up in her own right, being strong, loving and reliable, it turned out for me to be the best discovery of my adult life. The last time I looked at my mum's jumper it had a gold star badge on it; I wonder where she got that from?

Nothing Beautiful in this world is ever really lost. All things loved live in our hearts forever so before the lights go out on my journey so far, good night Catherine, I love you always, your wee brother Andrew.

Epilogue

When I decided over 12 years ago, including lots of times and for the best part of 4 years (at university) doing nothing about the idea, to start to write down some of my short stories, after being encouraged and inspired by many friends, family and colleagues, it was never my intention or understanding I would end up experiencing an emotional and challenging journey of personal reflection full of many roller-coaster type memories.

Then when I started to look at headings for the short stories I ended up with a big long list that started to look like and sound like a potential book. I had also decided its main focus would be about a young boy called (Nosher Bell) me, growing up in a place called Temple (scurvy-land) so the stories would start and end from the day I arrived to live there until the difficult and emotional final day I had to leave for good.

I soon realised all the times I would tell lots of the stories at lunch time in my work it was mainly funny stories all about the daft things we as young people experienced growing up in Temple, it was not about writing, exploring and reflecting on all the other challenging family related matters that start to contribute and shape who and what you are. I believe it's always much easer and within your comfort zone to write about funny situations and still capture the humour when translating these moments into written form, however, I found writing some of the more personal and emotive chapters of the book very challenging, a feeling of re-living the memory of some of the more hurtful and most difficult times of my young life and in a strange way left at times emotionally drained but eventually feeling a real sense of personal liberation by the experience.

I have never set out to settle old scores or embarrass anyone, or leave anyone out with this book, so I apologise if there is any offence caused by my reflective journey, everything I have written comes from how I understood it, through my eyes as I remember it, but most importantly through the eyes of a young Temple Scurvy boy, told, quite simply the way it was. I had and shared quite a few long laughs remembering a lot of the stories, especially from my school days and yes I have officially forgiven Fish for grassing me for dogging the school (only due to Betty's rolls 'n' choppy and Irn bru) .

Leaving Temple for good was a devastating time for me; it provided me with so many great memories and will always remain a very special place as will all the diverse characters that helped shape it and create a real sense of personal belonging, like part of a large extended family, I simply thank Temple for having me as one of its sons.

I had the opportunity to hang about with a lot of good mates, boys and lassies; we shared many great adventures and laughs growing up together, there are far two many to mention, but they will all know who they are. I thank all of them, we've all had our ups and downs, our moments in the past, but we all came through these times together to create a lasting friendship that shall always remain alive in my thoughts and memories.

So what of that Nosher bell, well maybe a lot more stories? I think the boy did ok, I decided when my dad left us, to choose to become a survivor and not a victim, I stopped work with my dad and got into youth work and then community work. I worked in local authority, social work services in Glasgow for 22 years as a community worker, worked in the housing sector and with adults with learning disabilities, challenging attitudes and changing hearts and minds within the local community.

Lost my fringe (hair) at 28, got to 40 odds and decided to leave it all behind and head for a new experience in Lanzarote, bought a wee cards and candy shop, been here for the past 2 years and now thinking about heading back home, but need to think long and hard about the weather and a reunion with direct debits.

If the ex head-teacher or teachers of St Ninians primary school are reading this book and remember that Andrew Bell, who gave you all that bother and was a bad influence at times in your school, well he ended up at Glasgow University and graduated with a degree, so he's making a decent go at life, against all the odds and to all the education boffs who write "if at first you don't succeed you won't succeed"... simply.............. You can all suck- seeds.

My dad did get re-married, sadly, his new wife Tina died suddenly a few years ago, he has 3 additional weans, Julie, John and Catherine, who are all great, they look after and love old Jude hornblower Bell very much, yes relationships and situations have at times difficult throughout the years, but I have always retained a good relationship with my dad and new family and for the record, have never hated my dad, at times in the past been disappointed with his actions and general lack of involvement with my family, but time, maturity and experience provides for a more understanding of how families and individual relationships work or not and respect that every story has another side to offer. It was also very important for me to respect my other family member's feelings and personal decisions related to the level and type of relationship they choose to have with my dad and not impose otherwise on them.

I met and fell in love with the girl up stairs, Wee Joyce Cameron; she set about slowly drawing me away from Temple for the right reasons and encouraging me to start to focus on my future, that time, we refer to as starting to grow up, stopping all the daft stuff (well most of it) everything positive I have achieved in my life since meeting Joyce is a real joint effort, she has given me direction, energy, belief and always supported me, standing by my side all the way, so simply and in a way no amount of words can express, thank you for all your support and for being my everlasting true love.

We have two beautiful grown up children of which I can't be any more proud of, Andrew (soldier) and Amanda (sparky), now both married to Laura and Riyad and 3 lovely grand-children Kenlyn, Anna Maria and (wee mini me) Lacey and soon another wee razzer fae Amanda (Leena).

A few friends of ours I have to mention, they have had to put up with all the stories, repeated time after time in different company and still managed to find laughter on most occasions, Mick and Mattie, Wilma and Debbie, Sandra, big Ricey-D and to Maurice my ex betting Christian pal for spotting me in the crowd and believing in my potential, thanks to you all.

So then there's Chrissie, my mum, she became the real strength and main inspiration for me writing this book, the depth of gratitude and love I have for my mum is off the scale, she abandoned her own dreams and aspirations, put her own personal life on permanent hold, to focus all her energy and effort, without making a fuss, into the struggle of bringing up all her children on her own. It's a real testimony to my mum's efforts when you look at all my sisters and brother to see how well they have done, and now with all their own lovely families to celebrate with and to be so proud of their continuous achievements.

The most important things in life are your family, friends, health, good humour and a positive attitude towards life. If you have these then you have everything!

If your feet are tired and weary

By

Andy Bell (aka) Nosher Bell

A childhood memory of a young boy growing up in the West of Glasgow...... inspired by the suggestion that the best days of your life are 'growing up'. For him, it was the importance of capturing many magical memories, ups and downs, happy and sad stories, but never a dull day and being brought up in a place blessed with characters, hard-working families and a neighbourhood that had a real strength of community, like a big extended family, associated for life, simply for living, growing up, or choosing to hang about Temple the land, known Simply to many as 'Temple Scurvy"

Printed in the United Kingdom by
Lightning Source UK Ltd., Milton Keynes
140320UK00001B/116/P